OPPOSING
VIEWPOINTS®
SERIES

Corporate
Social Responsibility

Other Books of Related Interest

Opposing Viewpoints Series

American Values

Community Policing

Outsourcing

Religious Liberty

At Issue Series

Are Unions Still Relevant?

Drones

Fracking

Is China's Economic Growth a Threat to America?

Current Controversies Series

Poverty and Homelessness

Social Security

Urban Sprawl

The Wage Gap

"Congress shall make no law ... abridging the freedom of speech, or of the press."

First Amendment to the US Constitution

The basic foundation of our democracy is the First Amendment guarantee of freedom of expression. The Opposing Viewpoints Series is dedicated to the concept of this basic freedom and the idea that it is more important to practice it than to enshrine it.

OPPOSING VIEWPOINTS® SERIES

Corporate Social Responsibility

Margaret Haerens and Lynn M. Zott, Book Editors

GREENHAVEN PRESS
A part of Gale, Cengage Learning

GALE
CENGAGE Learning·

Farmington Hills, Mich • San Francisco • New York • Waterville, Maine
Meriden, Conn • Mason, Ohio • Chicago

Elizabeth Des Chenes, *Director, Content Strategy*
Douglas Dentino, Manager, *New Product*

© 2014 Greenhaven Press, a part of Gale, Cengage Learning.

WCN: 01-100-101

Gale and Greenhaven Press are registered trademarks used herein under license.

For more information, contact:
Greenhaven Press
27500 Drake Rd.
Farmington Hills, MI 48331-3535
Or you can visit our Internet site at gale.cengage.com

For product information and technology assistance, contact us at

Gale Customer Support, 1-800-877-4253
For permission to use material from this text or product, submit all requests online at
www.cengage.com/permissions

Further permissions questions can be emailed to permissionrequest@cengage.com

Articles in Greenhaven Press anthologies are often edited for length to meet page requirements. In addition, original titles of these works are changed to clearly present the main thesis and to explicitly indicate the author's opinion. Every effort is made to ensure that Greenhaven Press accurately reflects the original intent of the authors. Every effort has been made to trace the owners of copyrighted material.

Cover image copyright © Caminoel/Shutterstock.com.

LIBRARY OF CONGRESS CATALOGING-IN-PUBLICATION DATA

Corporate social responsibility (Greenhaven Press) / Corporate social responsibility / Margaret Haerens and Lynn M. Zott, book editors.
    pages cm. -- (Opposing viewpoints)
    Includes bibliographical references and index.
    ISBN 978-0-7377-6652-3 (hardcover) -- ISBN 978-0-7377-6653-0 (pbk.)
    1. Social responsibility of business. 2. Corporate culture. 3. Corporations--Moral and ethical aspects. I. Haerens, Margaret. II. Zott, Lynn M. (Lynn Marie), 1969- III. Title.
    HD60.C69115 2014
    658.4'08--dc23
                                                        2013051274

Printed in the United States of America
1 2 3 4 5 6 7 18 17 16 15 14

Contents

Chapter 3: What Economic Issues Surround Corporate Social Responsibility?

Why Consider
Opposing Viewpoints?

"The only way in which a human being can make some approach to knowing the whole of a subject is by hearing what can be said about it by persons of every variety of opinion and studying all modes in which it can be looked at by every character of mind. No wise man ever acquired his wisdom in any mode but this."

John Stuart Mill

In our media-intensive culture it is not difficult to find differing opinions. Thousands of newspapers and magazines and dozens of radio and television talk shows resound with differing points of view. The difficulty lies in deciding which opinion to agree with and which "experts" seem the most credible. The more inundated we become with differing opinions and claims, the more essential it is to hone critical reading and thinking skills to evaluate these ideas. Opposing Viewpoints books address this problem directly by presenting stimulating debates that can be used to enhance and teach these skills. The varied opinions contained in each book examine many different aspects of a single issue. While examining these conveniently edited opposing views, readers can develop critical thinking skills such as the ability to compare and contrast authors' credibility, facts, argumentation styles, use of persuasive techniques, and other stylistic tools. In short, the Opposing Viewpoints Series is an ideal way to attain the higher-level thinking and reading skills so essential in a culture of diverse and contradictory opinions.

In addition to providing a tool for critical thinking, Opposing Viewpoints books challenge readers to question their own strongly held opinions and assumptions. Most people form their opinions on the basis of upbringing, peer pressure, and personal, cultural, or professional bias. By reading carefully balanced opposing views, readers must directly confront new ideas as well as the opinions of those with whom they disagree. This is not to argue simplistically that everyone who reads opposing views will—or should—change his or her opinion. Instead, the series enhances readers' understanding of their own views by encouraging confrontation with opposing ideas. Careful examination of others' views can lead to the readers' understanding of the logical inconsistencies in their own opinions, perspective on why they hold an opinion, and the consideration of the possibility that their opinion requires further evaluation.

Evaluating Other Opinions

To ensure that this type of examination occurs, Opposing Viewpoints books present all types of opinions. Prominent spokespeople on different sides of each issue as well as well-known professionals from many disciplines challenge the reader. An additional goal of the series is to provide a forum for other, less known, or even unpopular viewpoints. The opinion of an ordinary person who has had to make the decision to cut off life support from a terminally ill relative, for example, may be just as valuable and provide just as much insight as a medical ethicist's professional opinion. The editors have two additional purposes in including these less known views. One, the editors encourage readers to respect others' opinions—even when not enhanced by professional credibility. It is only by reading or listening to and objectively evaluating others' ideas that one can determine whether they are worthy of consideration. Two, the inclusion of such viewpoints encourages the important critical thinking skill of objectively evaluating an author's credentials and bias. This evaluation will illuminate an author's reasons for taking a particular stance on an issue and will aid in readers' evaluation of the author's ideas.

It is our hope that these books will give readers a deeper understanding of the issues debated and an appreciation of the complexity of even seemingly simple issues when good and honest people disagree. This awareness is particularly important in a democratic society such as ours in which people enter into public debate to determine the common good. Those with whom one disagrees should not be regarded as enemies but rather as people whose views deserve careful examination and may shed light on one's own.

Thomas Jefferson once said that "difference of opinion leads to inquiry, and inquiry to truth." Jefferson, a broadly educated man, argued that "if a nation expects to be ignorant and free . . . it expects what never was and never will be." As individuals and as a nation, it is imperative that we consider the opinions of others and examine them with skill and discernment. The Opposing Viewpoints Series is intended to help readers achieve this goal.

David L. Bender and Bruno Leone,
Founders

Introduction

> *"If our era is to be a renaissance of enlightened thinking that has an impact on the world, it must come from consumers owning their voices and using their leverage to encourage corporations and investors to embrace socially responsible capitalism."*
>
> —Simon Mainwaring,
> *"10 Actions Consumers Can Take to Reinvent Capitalism,"*
> Huffington Post, *June 7, 2011*

On the morning of April 24, 2013, an eight-story building known as the Rana Plaza collapsed in an industrial suburb of Dhaka, the capital city of Bangladesh. On its higher floors, the building had housed five garment factories that manufactured apparel for well-known American and European brands, including Walmart, Sears, The Children's Place, and Benetton. At the time of the collapse, more than three thousand workers were in the building. Several small children were also on-site, in nursery facilities used by working mothers who were on the job. Tragically, there was no chance for the men, women, and children in the building to escape. Many were trapped alive in the rubble. Soldiers, search-and-rescue teams, and civilians rushed to the scene, frantically trying to save as many people as possible.

These valiant efforts saved the lives of more than 2,500 people—many of whom stayed trapped for days until equipment and rescue teams could move heavy debris to free them. A number of workers did not survive: 1,129 bodies were recovered from the rubble. The Rana Plaza collapse is regarded as the deadliest garment-factory accident in history.

In the aftermath of the tragedy, the Bangladeshi media uncovered a number of shocking facts about the building, its owner, and its safety record. A day before the collapse occurred, a safety inspector had found significant cracks in Rana Plaza during a routine investigation. The inspector had issued a request that all the businesses in the building be closed and the workers evacuated for safety reasons. Although the businesses on the lower floor were immediately closed, the factories on the higher floors ignored the warnings and ordered their workers to report the next day as usual. It was that next morning that the building collapsed.

Public anger in Bangladesh and the world intensified when the media reported that the higher floors were never supposed to be used for factories in the first place. The architect who had designed the building revealed that the eight-story commercial building was supposed to house only shops and offices—not congested factories that utilized heavy equipment, which often vibrated the walls and floors. A number of experts later confirmed that the building was not strong enough to withstand the weight and vibration of numerous sewing machines and other heavy equipment. The head of the Bangladeshi Fire Service & Civil Defense reported that the upper floors had been built without a permit.

Public attention turned to the owner of the Rana Plaza, Sohel Rana, a well-connected politician and businessman. Rana and the five owners of the garment factories housed in the building were arrested by authorities. The building inspectors who had renewed permits for the garment factories, despite the fact that the building could not safely house them, were charged. The public was outraged at the avoidable tragedy, as well as the rampant corruption and cronyism that set the stage for the Rana Plaza collapse.

Just five months before the tragedy at Rana Plaza unfolded, a terrible fire at another garment factory, the Tazreen Fashion facility in Dhaka, had claimed the lives of 117 people and injured about 200 others. The fire was allegedly caused by an electrical problem, but it was the factory's lack of emergency exits and safety violations—such as padlocked exits and workers forced to stay in the building as the fire spread—that were directly responsible for the deaths of many men and women.

The Tazreen Fashion factory, like the garment manufacturers in the Rana Plaza building, made clothing for some of the top brand names in the United States and Europe. As investigators began to uncover the negligence, incompetence, corruption, and outright greed that led to both incidents, the global business community began to examine the role that multinational corporations played in the tragedies.

Bangladesh is the second-largest garment exporter in the world, with approximately 3.6 million men and women working in more than five thousand garment factories in and around urban centers. Like the Tazreen Fashion facility and the five garment manufacturers facilities located in Rana Plaza, most of these manufacturing centers have been allowed to function without basic safety standards, endangering the lives of their workers every day.

The Human Rights Watch, an international human rights organization, called on large multinational companies to ensure that Bangladeshi garment factories adhere to international labor and safety standards. "Global companies and consumers profit from cheap labor in Bangladesh, but do little to demand the most basic and humane conditions for those who toil on their behalf," stated Brad Adams, the Asia director at the Human Rights Watch. "It is time for companies to say that they will take no clothes from companies that do not meet minimum standards. Ignorance and cost no longer can be an excuse for some of the biggest companies in the world."[1]

Scott Nova, the executive director of the labor-rights group Worker Rights Consortium, also pointed out that the drive for greater corporate profit has led to dire consequences for workers in developing countries like Bangladesh. "The front-line responsibility is the government's, but the real power lies with Western brands and retailers, beginning with the biggest players: Walmart, H & M, Inditex, Gap and others," Nova asserted. "The price pressure these buyers put on factories undermines any prospect that factories will undertake the costly repairs and renovations that are necessary to make these buildings safe."[2]

A number of multinational corporations have expressed ignorance of specific factory conditions in Bangladesh and have pledged to promote stronger safety measures throughout their supply chains. In May 2013, officials from more than thirty multinational corporations, including Walmart, Gap, and H & M, met in Germany to formulate a plan to address the problems in Bangladesh, especially the need for stronger safety protections for workers in the garment industry. A handful of retailers, including the Anglo-Irish corporation Primark, have pledged funds for a compensation package for the families of the workers killed at Rana Plaza.

"We knew we were having clothes made in Rana Plaza—we announced that on the first day," remarked Paul Lister, Primark's general counsel. "When you know where your clothes are made, then you take responsibility for the results of where your clothes are being made. We have said very clearly that we would work to support the workers—and the families of the workers—in our supply chain."[3]

The authors of the viewpoints presented in *Opposing Viewpoints: Corporate Social Responsibility* explore the social responsibility of corporations in the following chapters: Should Corporations Practice Social Responsibility?, What Is the Goal of an Effective Corporate Social Responsibility Strategy?, What Economic Issues Surround Corporate Social Responsibility?, and Should Corporations Be Responsible for Health Insurance Coverage? The information in this volume will explore the efficacy and growing popularity of corporate social responsibility strategies, the most effective components of any social responsibility policy, and the recent debate over the role of business in US health insurance coverage.

Notes

1. Human Rights Watch, "Bangladesh: Tragedy Shows Urgency of Worker Protections," April 25, 2013. www.hrw.org.

2. Julfikar Ali Manik and Jim Yardley, "Building Collapse in Bangladesh Leaves Scores Dead," *New York Times*, April 24, 2013. www.nytimes.com.

3. "US Retailers Decline to Aid Tazreen, Rana Plaza Victims," Star Online Report, *The Daily Star*, November 23, 2013. www.thedailystar.net.

Should Corporations Practice Social Responsibility?

Chapter Preface

The concept of corporate social responsibility (CSR) can be traced back to the 1960s, when sweeping social and environmental movements began to influence the expectations consumers had of corporate behavior in the United States.

Activists began to launch campaigns to demand that corporations treat employees with respect and fairness, create programs or philanthropies to improve the community, and practice environmental sustainability. Consumers came to expect corporations to have moral, ethical, and philanthropic obligations to the local community and—in a larger sense—to the global community. Corporations began to invest time, manpower, and money in order to develop policies, practices, and philanthropic programs that addressed serious problems such as poverty, urban blight and crime, educational fairness, access to technology, and economic development in developing countries.

In many cases, CSR has made a real difference in communities and has improved the lives of employees, consumers, and others. Today, CSR strategies are standard in corporations all over the world.

As the concept of CSR emerged and corporations began to entertain the idea of adopting CSR policies, a number of major economists and business leaders scoffed at the idea. In 1962 the prominent American economist Milton Friedman expressed his views on CSR in his seminal study of economic capitalism, *Capitalism and Freedom*. "There is one and only one social responsibility of business—to use its resources and engage in activities designed to increase its profits," he wrote. By maximizing profits, companies could open more factories or stores and hire more people. Those added employees would stimulate the local economies and improve communities. Friedman's assertion—that the only responsibility of business was to its stakeholders through the maximization of profits—became a central tenet of late twentieth-century economic thought.

Yet as much as many business leaders and economists argued that corporations were only obligated to make money, consumers continued to hold corporations accountable for damaging and morally reprehensible environmental and social policies and practices. In the 1970s and 1980s, the global campaign against South Africa's apartheid policies utilized international boycotts of corporations that invested in or did business with South Africa. Over time, the country's white government was forced to change its racist policies and allow a more democratic system of government, confirming the growing power of human rights activists and their influence on corporate behavior.

Realizing the power of the consumer and unwilling to provoke further anti-corporate backlash, corporations began to respond to consumer concerns for greater accountability and better corporate behavior. In the 1990s CSR became an established part of corporate culture, influencing the ways corporations communicate with stakeholders and consumers and the ways in which businesses treat employees, the environment, and communities.

The emergence and growing importance of CSR in the global corporate community is explored in the following chapter, which examines the role of CSR in today's corporate culture. Viewpoints in the chapter discuss the relationship between economic capitalism, corporate behavior, and social responsibility and elucidate the debate over the US government's reaction to international CSR standards.

> *"Corporate responsibility is something, whilst not regulated, that all companies should practice and be in line with in the same way that they would comply with operations to licence and regulatory infrastructure."*

Corporate Social Responsibility Is an Essential Strategy in Today's Marketplace

Rose Schreiber

Rose Schreiber is a strategy and communications consultant. In the following viewpoint, she asserts that a vigorous, well-considered corporate social responsibility (CSR) strategy is crucial in today's competitive marketplace. She points out that knowledgeable customers have high expectations and demand that companies be responsible—from sourcing, to supply chain, to social engagement. Too many corporations, according to Schreiber, view CSR as optional, of little financial value, or engage in superficial strategies that aren't integrated into the entire business. Schreiber argues that those beliefs and practices are misguided. In the real world, she says, CSR involves finding collaborative solutions that benefit society, enhance a corporation's bottom line, and bring sustainability and responsible practices to all aspects of business.

As you read, consider the following questions:

1. According to the 2012 RepTrak 100 study cited in the viewpoint, what percentage of consumers believe that the top one hundred companies in terms of CSR efforts cannot be trusted?

2. What percentage of responders to the 2012 RepTrak 100 study cited in the viewpoint believes that the top 100 CSR companies are acting as good corporate citizens?

3. What does Schreiber view as a turning point in the CSR debate in the United Kingdom?

Having grown up in the 1990s I have watched the term 'corporate social responsibility' (CSR) grow and evolve. Whilst the anti-sweatshop movement of that decade may have marked the real beginning of an era of increasing concern for social causes[1] today, CSR has come to cover three kinds of responsibility: economic, environmental and social [2], covering issues of the workplace, human rights, the community and the marketplace.

A Growing Disconnect

Last week [September 2013] I attended a breakfast briefing with the UK Government Department of Business, Innovation and Skills (BIS) on the current call for views around CSR and what government, business and others can do in order to realise its full benefits. A big issue for all businesses in the UK, one would imagine that BIS are being swamped with replies from different stakeholders voicing their opinions on this highly topical, heavily publicised, issue. Yet, we were informed that responses to date have been few.

Surprised by this, I got thinking about the growing disconnect that continues to embody CSR: its existence is considered mandatory, yet its implementation appears optional. As such, this piecemeal application results in the overarching appearance of CSR as being 'fluffy', with financially debatable outcomes.

Firstly, despite its popularity, CSR is still thought of, by many, as 'soft', 'left-wing', at best 'optional', at worst done 'for the sake of appearances'. This has been repeatedly shown by surveys that demonstrate that even where companies spend millions on CSR activities, consumers are sceptical of their intentions and believe a respective type of 'green washing' is at work. As the 2012 RepTrak 100 study shows us, despite being the top 100 companies in terms of CSR efforts, 4% of consumers believe they are 'absolutely not to be trusted' and a huge 60% aren't sure. Indeed, only 6% of consumers considered these companies to be acting as strong and good corporate citizens.[3] This has, as Kasper Nielsen from the Reputation Institute explains, left many believing CSR is dead, and that from a reputational improvement point of view, it simply doesn't work.

The Financial Value of CSR

Secondly, the entire premise on which CSR stands has been overtaken by the argument on whether or not it can be linked to financial value and a return on investment for the company involved. Pinpointing the financial value of CSR continues to be the overriding issue amongst economists, businessmen and philanthropists, and there appears to be no one answer. The expectation that companies can profit by serving the greater social good is being scrutinised down to the last penny. The view proclaimed by Milton Friedman [American economist] in 1970 that companies undertaking CSR initiatives do so to the detriment of shareholder value, is still shared by many. In fact, it has recently been argued that whilst CSR expenditures

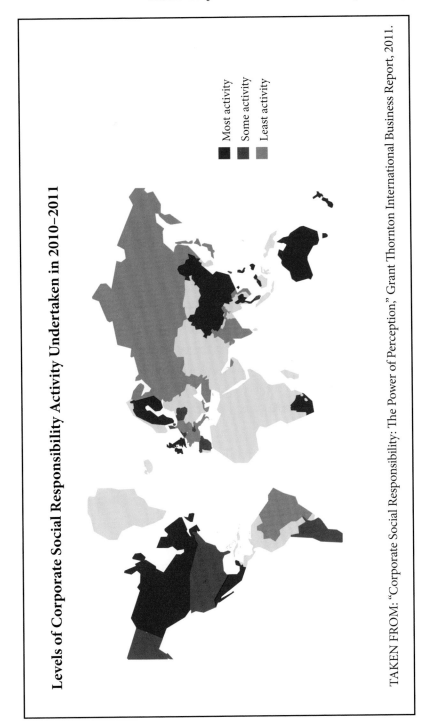

Levels of Corporate Social Responsibility Activity Undertaken in 2010–2011

Most activity

Some activity

Least activity

TAKEN FROM: "Corporate Social Responsibility: The Power of Perception," Grant Thornton International Business Report, 2011.

typically destroy shareholder value, when it does add value, it does so because that very CSR expenditure is seen as a precursor to future financial performance.[4] "To put it simply, CSR is what 'rich' companies do!"[5] This viewpoint is further exhausted by the confusion that many have in distinguishing between CSR, philanthropy, environmental disclosure and sustainability.

However, expectations in both the B2C [business-to-customer] and B2B [business-to-business] market have changed so much that corporations are now essentially required to adopt corporate social responsibility programmes to remain viable, [but] the rhetoric and actions on CSR should go beyond the fluff and the financial impact, and rather focus on how to ensure that it is integrated across the supply business chain.

Corporate responsibility is something, whilst not regulated, that all companies should practice and be in line with in the same way that they would comply with operations to licence and regulatory infrastructure. Corporate responsibility is not [an] option. In today's world, driven by high consumer expectations, being responsible from sourcing to supply chain to social engagement is a given. Finding the most sustainable way to do this is what the debate should now focus on.

It is easy to see why many feel that with regards to CSR, they are in a lose-lose situation in the eyes of their consumers and/or investors. In an environment which is financially challenging—where many companies may feel intimidated and financially ill-equipped to undertake and invest fully in CSR—the easy option is to apply it as a charitable add-on, a narrowly defined marketing function segregated from the rest of the business.[6] However, this is the very action of 'showing', as opposed to 'doing', that blights CSR and positions it as a 'fluffy', financially fruitless, undertaking.

A Turning Point

Thankfully though, help does appear to be on the way and I think it is great to see that the government are calling for these views and best practice examples on corporate responsibility. Hopefully, by engaging with a wider audience, including leading companies that succeed and profit from CSR (because they apply the same rigor on it as they do other core business priorities[7]), this call for views can bring about significant key learnings for everyone on the benefits of corporate responsibility. Indeed, I think this call marks an evolution in the CSR debate. Corporate responsibility these days is about finding solutions that benefit society and the company itself, collaboration among interested parties in the quest to learn from each other, being smart with the budget available, and learning from best practice in order to ensure sustainable thorough implementation. By companies communicating what they have done and what this means for society and their long term profitability, the image of CSR is going to shift towards a closed loop strategy which delivers added value and underpins this shift from philanthropy/doing-good to sustainable business practices.

Notes

1. Micheletti and Stolle 162.

2. http://www.xing.com/net/csr/csr-strategie-1175/the-birth-of-csr-1287154.

3. Is CSR dead? Or just mismanaged? http://www.forbes.com/sites/forbesinsights/2012/12/11/is-csr-dead-or-just-mismanaged.

4. Pinpointing the Value in CSR by Thomas Lys. James Naughton and Clare Wang. Kellogg School of Management at North-western University: http://insight.kellogg.northwestern.edu/article/pinpointing_the_value_in_csr.

5. Ibid.

6. https://www.devex.com/en/news/want-better-csr-companies-should-try-good-old/80796.

7. Is CSR dead? Or just mismanaged? http://www.forbes.com/sites/forbesinsights/2012/12/11/is-csr-dead-or-just-mismanaged.

> "CSR [Corporate Social Responsibility] remains a quick route to corporate gloss."

CSR: Social Good or Marketing Ploy?

Sudeep Chakravarti

Sudeep Chakravarti is an author and business columnist for Live Mint. *In the following viewpoint, he elucidates his opposition to a recent bill passed by the Indian government that mandates corporate social responsibility (CSR) for businesses of a certain size and profitability. Chakravarti maintains the state has little business trying to impose CSR on corporate India in light of its own record of corruption and political and administrative inefficiency. Another problem, he argues, is that CSR has been hijacked and employed as little more than a cynical public relations strategy, often used to provide a corporate gloss for gasping and troubled corporations. CSR can obscure a corporation's true motives and mask its bad behavior, according to Chakravarti. Hypocritical corporations utilizing CSR in these cynical ways must be exposed in order for the strategy's idealistic goals to be fully realized, he concludes.*

As you read, consider the following questions:

1. How does Chakravarti compare China and India's geo-political strategies?

2. When did the bill mandating corporate social responsi-bility pass in the Lok Sabha [the lower house of the In-dian Parliament], according to Chakravarti?

3. What does Chakravarti view as ironic about India's min-ister of state for corporate affairs Sachin Pilot's meeting with Indian industry leaders in December 2012?

The delusion of "soft" power can mask reality. Take geo-politics. China goes about its "string of pearls" approach for extending areas of influence with massive strategic invest-ment and strategic arm-twisting. "Soft" India typically offers limp festivals extolling Bollywood fare, tandoori chicken, tea, instant yoga, and exhortations to maintain "traditional cul-tural ties" that have little meaning in hard-nosed power plays. We all know China is continents ahead.

Perhaps there is a lesson in hard application of "soft" power from India's business community. For instance, many wield the blade of corporate social responsibility (CSR) with such finesse that it often makes CSR—the acronym freshly in-fused with life and controversy after the government's move towards the past year-end to mandate this activity for busi-nesses of a certain size and record of profitability—into a cynical engine of growth. CSR has for long been a useful weapon in marketing arsenals; it is viewed through the un-emotional calculus of the quickest return on investment, even as a tool to mask dubious records in corporate governance.

And so, mandating CSR in the Companies Bill, passed in the Lok Sabha last month, without greater scrutiny of corpo-rate behaviour by shareholders, investor watchdogs, media and activists will likely prove hollow.

This has nothing to do with my personal conviction that the state has little business trying to impose CSR on corporate India when its own record in implementing development projects on account of political and administrative inefficiency and corruption is counted among the worst in the world. Indeed, when the minister of state for corporate affairs Sachin Pilot met a group of representatives from industry in early December to soften them up for the Bill in parliamentary transit, he could hardly have missed the irony. The minister spoke of the need for "visible social intervention" by business. An official dissemination of the meeting was almost school-marmish: "As a pointer to socially relevant activities, the minister drew attention to the need to give priority to hygiene and sanitation in rural areas particularly for provision of toilets in girls' schools in government-run and government-aided institutions in the secondary and senior secondary sectors with water conservation technologies . . ." (Query: What on earth have the central and state governments been doing these past 65 years with public funds? Not just for providing sanitation in schools, but to ensure education and sanitation in general, let alone other socio-economic imperatives?)

It has also nothing to do with my personal conviction—mirroring that of many other critics—that it will, sooner than later, be too tempting for government to keep its hands away from the special purpose vehicle that seeks to aggregate such CSR funds, and turn the monitoring agency into another cash-eating government monster of deliberate ineptitude. In all likelihood, such a system will collapse with only public sector undertakings continuing to bear the cross of the government's failures in development. My concern is more basic. It stems from the root of CSR, which grew into a form of enlightened corporate behaviour not because business leaders discovered themselves to be saints after acquiring their millions, but quite apart from philanthropy, as a legitimate, "new-age" extension of the art of public relations.

CSR remains a quick route to corporate gloss. It permits a corporation to be seen as an active ingredient in developing national sporting infrastructure—shooting, mountaineering—while suppressing news of culpability—of, say, several people killed and injured to acquire land for its projects. It permits a corporation to establish a CSR footprint in an area in which it is actively engaged in acquiring land by establishing a rural health clinic, rather than pursuing a less cynical CSR plan that would have established that clinic on account of that clinic being needed anyway. It permits a corporation to spend millions of rupees to maintain gardens—claiming it as CSR activity—at the main airport of a state in which it has ongoing and future business interests. Or plaster streets with posters and billboards that show smiling children benefiting from a handful of rural schools it funds, while at the same time attempting to curb using, say, the state's heavy-handed police power, growing farmers' agitations against its coal or iron ore mine, or power plant, or special economic zone, in said rural area.

The hypocrisy embedded in the practice of CSR needs to first be addressed. We need to continually expose the often noxious mix of corporate affairs, corporate governance, CSR, and public relations. Or it will remain yet another ticket to take citizens and shareholders for a ride.

"Very simply, in cases where private profits and public interests are aligned, the idea of corporate social responsibility is irrelevant: Companies that simply do everything they can to boost profits will end up increasing social welfare."

The Case Against Corporate Social Responsibility

Aneel Karnani

Aneel Karnani is an associate professor of strategy at the University of Michigan's Stephen M. Ross School of Business. In the following viewpoint, he deems the idea that corporations should act in a socially responsible manner as fundamentally flawed; although it is an appealing concept, he says, corporations will always pursue policies to boost profits, sometimes at the expense of socially and environmentally beneficial strategies. At other times, Karnani indicates, profits and the public interest align. Karnani asserts that business executives must focus on their fiduciary responsibilities to shareholders first and foremost, and any executive that places corporate social responsibility (CSR) strategy ahead of profits will likely be replaced. He argues that there are more effective ways to strike a balance between profits and being socially responsible, including government regulation, watchdogs and advocates, self-regulation, and making it financially attractive for corporations to do the right thing.

As you read, consider the following questions:

1. What does Karnani cite as the reason corporations have not done more to solve the persistent problem of poverty?

2. According to Karnani, how can government regulation encourage good corporate behavior?

3. What environmental organization does the author cite as having success in lobbying for environmental protections and sustainability strategies?

Can companies do well by doing good? Yes—sometimes.

But the idea that companies have a responsibility to act in the public interest and will profit from doing so is fundamentally flawed.

Large companies now routinely claim that they aren't in business just for the profits, that they're also intent on serving some larger social purpose. They trumpet their efforts to produce healthier foods or more fuel-efficient vehicles, conserve energy and other resources in their operations, or otherwise make the world a better place. Influential institutions like the Academy of Management and the United Nations, among many others, encourage companies to pursue such strategies.

It's not surprising that this idea has won over so many people—it's a very appealing proposition. You can have your cake and eat it too!

But it's an illusion, and a potentially dangerous one.

Very simply, in cases where private profits and public interests are aligned, the idea of corporate social responsibility is irrelevant: Companies that simply do everything they can to boost profits will end up increasing social welfare. In circumstances in which profits and social welfare are in direct opposition, an appeal to corporate social responsibility will almost always be ineffective, because executives are unlikely to act voluntarily in the public interest and against shareholder interests.

Irrelevant or ineffective, take your pick. But it's worse than that. The danger is that a focus on social responsibility will delay or discourage more-effective measures to enhance social welfare in those cases where profits and the public good are at odds. As society looks to companies to address these problems, the real solutions may be ignored.

Well and Good

To get a better fix on the irrelevance or ineffectiveness of corporate social responsibility efforts, let's first look at situations where profits and social welfare are in synch.

Consider the market for healthier food. Fast-food outlets have profited by expanding their offerings to include salads and other options designed to appeal to health-conscious consumers. Other companies have found new sources of revenue in low-fat, whole-grain and other types of foods that have grown in popularity. Social welfare is improved. Everybody wins.

Similarly, auto makers have profited from responding to consumer demand for more fuel-efficient vehicles, a plus for the environment. And many companies have boosted profits while enhancing social welfare by reducing their energy consumption and thus their costs.

But social welfare isn't the driving force behind these trends. Healthier foods and more fuel-efficient vehicles didn't become so common until they became profitable for their makers. Energy conservation didn't become so important to many companies until energy became more costly. These companies are benefiting society while acting in their own interests; social activists urging them to change their ways had little impact. It is the relentless maximization of profits, not a commitment to social responsibility, that has proved to be a boon to the public in these cases.

Unfortunately, not all companies take advantage of such opportunities, and in those cases both social welfare and profits suffer. These companies have one of two problems: Their executives are either incompetent or are putting their own interests ahead of the company's long-term financial interests. For instance, an executive might be averse to any risk, including the development of new products, that might jeopardize the short-term financial performance of the company and thereby affect his compensation, even if taking that risk would improve the company's longer-term prospects.

An appeal to social responsibility won't solve either of those problems. Pressure from shareholders for sustainable growth in profitability can. It can lead to incompetent managers being replaced and to a realignment of incentives for executives, so that their compensation is tied more directly to the company's long-term success.

When There's a Choice

Still, the fact is that while companies sometimes can do well by doing good, more often they can't. Because in most cases, doing what's best for society means sacrificing profits.

This is true for most of society's pervasive and persistent problems; if it weren't, those problems would have been solved long ago by companies seeking to maximize their profits. A prime example is the pollution caused by manufacturing. Reducing that pollution is costly to the manufacturers, and that eats into profits. Poverty is another obvious example. Companies could pay their workers more and charge less for their products, but their profits would suffer.

So now what? Should executives in these situations heed the call for corporate social responsibility even without the allure of profiting from it?

You can argue that they should. But you shouldn't expect that they will.

Executives are hired to maximize profits; that is their responsibility to their company's shareholders. Even if executives wanted to forgo some profit to benefit society, they could expect to lose their jobs if they tried—and be replaced by managers who would restore profit as the top priority. The movement for corporate social responsibility is in direct opposition, in such cases, to the movement for better corporate governance, which demands that managers fulfill their fiduciary duty to act in the shareholders' interest or be relieved of their responsibilities. That's one reason so many companies talk a great deal about social responsibility but do nothing—a tactic known as greenwashing.

Managers who sacrifice profit for the common good also are in effect imposing a tax on their shareholders and arbitrarily deciding how that money should be spent. In that sense they are usurping the role of elected government officials, if only on a small scale.

Privately owned companies are a different story. If an owner-operated business chooses to accept diminished profit in order to enhance social welfare, that decision isn't being imposed on shareholders. And, of course, it is admirable and desirable for the leaders of successful public companies to use some of their personal fortune for charitable purposes, as many have throughout history and many do now. But those leaders shouldn't presume to pursue their philanthropic goals with shareholder money. Indeed, many shareholders themselves use significant amounts of the money they make from their investments to help fund charities or otherwise improve social welfare.

This is not to say, of course, that companies should be left free to pursue the greatest possible profits without regard for the social consequences. But, appeals to corporate social responsibility are not an effective way to strike a balance between profits and the public good.

The Power of Regulation

So how can that balance best be struck?

The ultimate solution is government regulation. Its greatest appeal is that it is binding. Government has the power to enforce regulation. No need to rely on anyone's best intentions.

But government regulation isn't perfect, and it can even end up *reducing* public welfare because of its cost or inefficiency. The government also may lack the resources and competence to design and administer appropriate regulations, particularly for complex industries requiring much specialized knowledge. And industry groups might find ways to influence regulation to the point where it is ineffective or even ends up benefiting the industry at the expense of the general population.

Outright corruption can make the situation even worse. What's more, all the problems of government failure are exacerbated in developing countries with weak and often corrupt governments.

Still, with all their faults, governments are a far more effective protector of the public good than any campaign for corporate social responsibility.

Watchdogs and Advocates

Civil society also plays a role in constraining corporate behavior that reduces social welfare, acting as a watchdog and advocate. Various nonprofit organizations and movements provide a voice for a wide variety of social, political, environmental, ethnic, cultural and community interests.

The Rainforest Action Network, for example, is an organization that agitates, often quite effectively, for environmental protection and sustainability. Its website states, "Our campaigns leverage public opinion and consumer pressure to turn the public stigma of environmental destruction into a business nightmare for any American company that refuses to adopt responsible environmental policies." That's quite a different approach from trying to convince executives that they should do what's best for society because it's the right thing to do and won't hurt their bottom line.

Overall, though, such activism has a mixed track record, and it can't be relied on as the primary mechanism for imposing constraints on corporate behavior—especially in most developing countries, where civil society lacks adequate resources to exert much influence and there is insufficient awareness of public issues among the population.

Self-Control

Self-regulation is another alternative, but it suffers from the same drawback as the concept of corporate social responsibility: Companies are unlikely to voluntarily act in the public interest at the expense of shareholder interests.

But self-regulation can be useful. It tends to promote good practices and target specific problems within industries, impose lower compliance costs on businesses than government regulation, and offer quick, low-cost dispute-resolution procedures. Self-regulation can also be more flexible than government regulation, allowing it to respond more effectively to changing circumstances.

The challenge is to design self-regulation in a manner that emphasizes transparency and accountability, consistent with what the public expects from government regulation. It is up to the government to ensure that any self-regulation meets that standard. And the government must be prepared to step in and impose its own regulations if the industry fails to police itself effectively.

Financial Calculation

In the end, social responsibility is a financial calculation for executives, just like any other aspect of their business. The only sure way to influence corporate decision making is to impose an unacceptable cost—regulatory mandates, taxes, punitive fines, public embarrassment—on socially unacceptable behavior.

Pleas for corporate social responsibility will be truly embraced only by those executives who are smart enough to see that doing the right thing is a byproduct of their pursuit of profit. And that renders such pleas pointless.

| *"The efforts to set well-coordinated and systematic standards for CSR [corporate social responsibility] are definitely necessary."*

US Corporations Should Embrace International Corporate Social Responsibility Standards

Mahesh Chandra

Mahesh Chandra is an associate professor of information technology and quantitative methods at the Frank G. Zarb School of Business at Hofstra University. In the following viewpoint, he underscores the value of establishing an international set of standards for the practice of corporate social responsibility (CSR). He makes particular reference to the 2010 publication of the ISO 26000, created by the International Organization for Standardization (ISO). The ISO 26000, Chandra explains, is based on the principles of accountability, transparency, ethical conduct, legal compliance, and a recognition of stakeholder's interests. More

Mahesh Chandra, "ISO Standards from Quality to Environment to Corporate Social Responsibility and Their Implications for Global Companies," *The Journal of International Business and Law*, vol. 14, March 30, 2011, pp. 111–113. Copyright © 2011 by The Hofstra University School of Law. All rights reserved. Reproduced by permission.

than four hundred experts were consulted in its formulation. Chandra suggests that international CSR standards are necessary and represent a big step forward in the area of CSR.

As you read, consider the following questions:

1. According to Chandra, who made the earliest recorded reference to stakeholders?

2. Who does Chandra cite as one of the first people to champion the idea of corporate social responsibility guidelines?

3. What is the membership of the ISO?

There is no single universal framework describing the activities that are part of CSR [corporate social responsibility] initiatives. The difficulty stems from the varied assumptions under which CSR principles and activities are developed. Moreover, CSR also appears to be geographically and culturally driven; that is, companies' activities and society's demands on companies vary from country to country. For example, in Europe the public demands that companies be more responsive to environmental concerns, whereas in the United States firms are driven by increasing shareholder value.

The Stakeholder Concept

The concerns of stakeholders and corporate concerns about satisfying their interests are probably less than a hundred years old. The earliest recorded reference to stakeholders was made by E. Merrick Dodd, Jr., a Harvard law professor, who, based on information from General Electric executives, referred to shareholders, employees, customers, and the general public as part of the stakeholders of a company. The formal introduction of the stakeholders concept, though not the name, into the management literature is credited to William R. Dill, based on a 1958 Scandinavian field study. Other equally important figures in the evolution of the stakeholder concept and general stakeholder theory are Edward R. Freeman and James D. Thompson, who formalized the stakeholder principles and wrote extensively about them. Stakeholders are defined as "an individual or group, inside or outside the organization that has a stake in and can influence an organization's performance."

According to the stakeholder theory, every company should identify individuals or groups whose involvement is critical to a company's success and should make every attempt to satisfy each of these individual's or group's needs and interests. Moreover, the company must be viewed through numerous interactions with its stakeholders. The theory implies that as it strives to create shareholder wealth, a company should also meet the expectations of its employees, customers, and suppliers; the community it operates in; and any other individual or group that it affects. The theory does not imply that any one stakeholder is more important than the others and hence assumes that a company and its managers should strive to satisfy the interests and concerns of all. From a practical standpoint, the level of satisfaction that needs to be delivered to the stakeholders is not defined, and herein lays the conundrum for executives, practitioners, academicians, and community representatives. Is it possible to fully satisfy the needs and interests of all concerned?

Various CSR Standards

To govern the varying philosophies and theories that surround the CSR issues, various government agencies, international organizations, and industry associations have developed standards for businesses to follow. In addition, a few countries have developed regulations related to CSR, and the companies operating in these countries are expected to report CSR-related activities to the government as required by law. Many of the country-specific laws, standards, and guidelines that are developed by nongovernmental agencies are meant to encourage and promote good practices in the areas of human rights, labor, the environment, and anticorruption. One of the early proponents of having guidelines for corporate social responsibility is the quality guru Edward Deming, who in 1986 proposed a fourteen-point checklist for companies to follow that, alludes to CSR.

International organizations' efforts in the area of CSR include the Global Reporting Initiative by the United Nations through the Global Compact unit, and the Organization for Economic Cooperation and Development [OECD] guidelines for companies that have to file CSR activity reports to these agencies. Furthermore, a few assessment devices have been developed to report CSR activities, such as the implementation of basic workplace rights developed by Social Accountability International (SA 8000) and procedures for environmental management developed by ISO [the International Organization for Standardization] (ISO 14000). Finally, industries such as mining and chemicals require voluntary compliance with industry-driven CSR initiatives.

Of all the various voluntary reporting that companies must do in regard to CSR activities, probably the Global Reporting Initiative is the most comprehensive. It includes elements of ISO 14000, SA 8000, and the OECD codes of conduct.

Corporate Social Responsibility and ISO 26000

As discussed previously, there are already many CSR standards and monitoring agencies in existence. The introduction of the ISO standards [known as ISO 26000] is meant not to add to the confusion of the existing slew of standards, but to add value to the current standards and have an organization known for its systems and international scope introduce a set of standards that follows its successful previous generation of standards on quality and sustainability. It is hoped that ISO 26000 will provide guidance to all types of organizations around the world. This includes business organizations (both goods and services), not-for-profit organizations, governmental organizations, and nongovernmental organizations. Some of the beneficial uses of the ISO 26000 standards are:

- A harmonization tool for current standards

- A practical tool for small and medium-size enterprises

- A marketing tool for businesses

- A platform for stakeholder groups

The basic principles of the ISO 26000 standards are as follows:

- Respect for and adherence to international norms of behavior

- Compliance with the current laws

- Recognition of stakeholders' interests

- Accountability

- Transparency

- Ethical conduct

- Respect for fundamental rights

Because ISO's international position is unique as a UN-recognized body, it is in the best position to integrate the current norms, indices, declarations, conventions, and codes. Moreover, ISO's membership of 157 countries with 110 developing country members provides it with an opportunity to establish and integrate the current codes. The purposes of the ISO 26000 standards are as follows:

- To agree on a universally accepted system of standards on CSR

What Is ISO 26000?

Business and organizations do not operate in a vacuum. Their relationship to the society and environment in which they operate is a critical factor in their ability to continue to operate effectively. It is also increasingly being used as a measure of their overall performance.

ISO 26000 provides guidance on how businesses and organizations can operate in a socially responsible way. This means acting in an ethical and transparent way that contributes to the health and welfare of society.

ISO 26000 provides guidance rather than requirements, so it cannot be certified unlike some other well-known ISO standards. Instead, it helps clarify what social responsibility is, helps businesses and organizations translate principles into effective actions and shares best practices relating to social responsibility, globally. It is aimed at all types of organizations regardless of their activity, size or location.

The standard was launched in 2010 following five years of negotiations between many different stakeholders across the world. Representatives from government, NGOs, industry, consumer groups and labour organizations around the world were involved in its development, which means it represents an international consensus.

"ISO 26000—Social Responsibility,"
International Organization for Standardization, 2013.

- To connect the various codes currently in existence to the ISO 26000 codes and to benefit executives in their daily management of organizations

- To build on the previously established codes, such as ISO 9000, ISO 14000, to assist various organizations in managing their operations

The ISO 26000 series was created over a six-year period with more than four hundred experts from eighty countries participating in the development of the standards. In addition, 60 experts from 34 liaison organizations also took part in the development process. Equally important was the participation of international organizations such as the International Labor Organization, the Organization for Economic Cooperation and Development, and the United Nations Global Compact.

Major Issues and Concerns for ISO 26000

The efforts to set well-coordinated and systematic standards for CSR are definitely necessary. If ISO 26000 succeeds, as have previous ISO standards, great strides will have been made in the area of CSR. But, unlike previous ISO standards, which were easily embraced by businesses and consumers, the CSR issue is a bit more complex and holds contradictory benefits for the parties concerned. For example, are the concerns of the various stakeholders equal? In other words, should investors sacrifice their returns and invest in community projects that might benefit a few stakeholders? Another issue is the question of who will bear the financial cost of adopting CSR initiatives. At the present time, many businesses deem allocation of funds to assist communities (building schools and libraries, donating food and medicines) or earmarking funds for cleanup of the environment as fulfilling CSR. In many instances, these companies publish detailed reports on their CSR initiatives in their annual reports so as to report a line item in their income statements to reflect the cost associated with their CSR initiatives as part of their business operations. Unlike quality issues, the issues that govern CSR are more varied and have no single thread that runs through them; hence, it is much more difficult to standardize.

In spite of the above concerns there is a general consensus among all parties concerned that a streamlined and well-coordinated set of CSR standards will benefit a majority.

A Welcome Standard

The ISO standards have definitely helped businesses, government agencies, and the world's masses receive an acceptable quality of goods and services. Additionally, ISO has acted as a voice for concerned citizens in macro-areas such as sustainability and the environment. After a successful introduction and worldwide acceptance of the ISO 9000 quality standards, ISO was equally successful in introducing standards and certification for the ISO 14000 series, which governed the environment. Now ISO has ventured into the area of CSR, probably a more complex and definitely a more far-reaching aspect of business than the previous undertakings.

The ISO 26000 is a worthy and promising standard. It has been undertaken under the guidance of many other organizations, agencies, and stakeholders representing a wide group of interests. The process seems to be transparent and participative and has taken into consideration the issue that the topic concerns a variety of constituents. The ISO has definitely answered the legitimacy issue through its previous successes and in the objective way it has approached the issue. The ISO 26000 standard definitely adds value to the existing CSR standards. Also, to ensure participation and maintain standards, it is important that this series also require third-party certification.

> "Governments that understand the ben-
> efits of the free market, as well as the
> business community, should resist this
> new radical CSR [corporate social re-
> sponsibility] agenda."

US Corporations Should Oppose International Corporate Social Responsibility Standards

James M. Roberts and Andrew W. Markley

*James M. Roberts is the research fellow for economic freedom
and growth at the Heritage Foundation. Andrew W. Markley is
chair and professor, Department of Business, at City Grove College. In the following viewpoint, they recommend that the United
States resist attempts to impose radical corporate social responsibility (CSR) standards, particularly the pernicious ISO 26000,
adopted by the International Organization for Standardization
(ISO). Roberts and Markley argue that the ISO 26000 redefines
the role of business in the social, economic, and environmental
arenas and seeks to make corporations adhere to "international*

norms of behavior." Many of these international standards, Roberts and Markley explain, are taken from treaties and conventions that the United States does not participate in or never ratified. Although these standards are voluntary now, the authors contend that opponents of free enterprise and other activists seek to make them permanent. This, they conclude, would be toxic to American businesses and must be opposed by everyone who believes in the power of the free market.

As you read, consider the following questions:

1. When was the ISO 26000 adopted by the ISO?

2. When was the UN Global Compact introduced?

3. What is the approximate total of United Nation's conventions, recommendations, treaties, reports, codes, and guidelines cited in the ISO 26000?

Until recently, proponents of corporate social responsibility (CSR) promoted it as a set of voluntary standards that, if adopted, would allow private companies to boast of their good stewardship of communities' resources. Many companies were all too happy to sign on to this movement as a public relations strategy to offset the ever-growing demands by government on the private sector. Sensing opportunity, CSR activists (whose ultimate goal is generally to tax private capital to increase the size and scope of government) have upped the ante and are ramping up their CSR demands.

This new CSR push is an attempt to redefine the very purpose of business by asserting so-called triple-bottom-line obligations of companies to deliver (1) economic, (2) social, and (3) environmental "returns" to justify a theoretical "license to operate" granted to them by society. Moreover, advocates of the new CSR are pushing to impose mandated standards instead of voluntary initiatives, assert comprehensive obligations in place of targeted projects, and require highly structured reporting in place of flexible communications.

ISO 26000

In 2010, for example, the International Organization for Standardization (ISO)—a nongovernmental organization founded in 1947 and based in Geneva, Switzerland, which sets international standards for doing business—adopted new CSR standards called "ISO 26000." Advertised as "voluntary" guidelines, the 100-page ISO 26000 is one of the most comprehensive expressions of the new CSR philosophy to date. It defines social responsibility in terms of complying with "international norms of behavior" in the social, economic, and environmental spheres.

This is a case of "buyers beware" for private companies. It is rare in CSR materials that its advocates stipulate which rights or status business owners have in this new bargain. Though words such as "stakeholder" appear frequently in CSR literature, "shareholder" and "owner" do not.

Governments that understand the benefits of the free market, as well as the business community, should resist this new radical CSR agenda. Regrettably, the Obama Administration is setting up an entire government bureaucracy to encourage and oversee the adoption of the CSR agenda.

The Administration has recently established the Stakeholder Advisory Board on the U.S. National Contact Point for the Organization for Economic Cooperation and Development (OECD) Guidelines for Multinational Enterprises, and a new office for the U.S. National Contact Point in the State Department's Bureau of Economic and Business Affairs. President Barack Obama should reverse those recent actions and Congress should block the use of any U.S. contributions to the OECD that fund programs that will institutionalize CSR activities in member state governments.

The New CSR Agenda: Redefining the Purpose of Business

Demands for corporate social responsibility have become louder over the past 20 years. During that time, a rich literature of advice for "doing well by doing good" has developed in the corporate world. Impatient CSR advocates, finding the corporate world too slow in adopting their agenda, found willing allies in international organizations that allegedly promote human rights and economic development within the United Nations bureaucracy. One early CSR effort was called the U.N. Global Compact, a statement introduced in 1999 that prescribed 10 "voluntary" principles that businesses could sign on to in exchange for the right to use the U.N.'s "We Support the Global Compact" logo in their advertising. The principles promote long-standing U.N. human rights, labor, environment, and anti-corruption standards. The first principle states: "Businesses should support and respect the protection of internationally proclaimed human rights." The second principle states that businesses should "make sure that they are not complicit in human rights abuses."

However, progressives and other CSR advocates are now pushing a new generation of radical and aggressive standards, principles, and strategies. The new CSR mentality seeks, at its core, to redefine the very purpose of business. The definition of CSR has increasingly cast aside the traditional focus of corporate management's responsibility to the firm's owners and investors and, instead, coalesces around what proponents assert is a triple-bottom-line obligation of companies to deliver not only economic, but social and environmental "returns" to their communities in order to justify a license to operate. In addition, the new concept of CSR seeks to change the focus from voluntary initiatives to mandated standards, from targeted projects to comprehensive obligations, and from flexible communications to highly structured reporting.

Advocates of this new CSR agenda believe that society is facing unprecedented challenges, and that, thus, the very definition of business must change to meet these challenges. Longtime CSR advocate and writer John Elkington asserts that the world is approaching an "environmental precipice" in which the very existence of life on planet Earth is threatened by global warming and ozone depletion. Harvard professors Michael Porter and Mark Kramer claim that, "[t]he capitalist system is under siege. In recent years business has increasingly been viewed as a major cause of social, environmental, and economic problems." They claim that this means nothing less than "creating a new conception of capitalism." Make no mistake, mere philanthropy or engaging in selective projects to benefit local communities will not satisfy the requirements of the new CSR agenda.

A Flawed Concept

Not only are these new CSR concepts fundamentally flawed, but in their rush to promote, expand, and institutionalize statist policies, CSR advocates have routinely failed to acknowledge the massive and glowing thicket of regulations that already form part of the modern regulatory state. As *The Economist* explained in 2005, CSR proponents assert, "It will no longer do for a company to go quietly about its business, telling no lies and breaking no laws, selling things that people want, and making money. That is so passé." However, legal compliance is no simple matter in the modern regulatory state. In this description, both the volume and complexity of regulatory laws—from environmental to employment, labor union, consumer protection, and antitrust—are completely ignored.

In his excellent 2008 book *Capitalism with Chinese Characteristics*, Yasheng Huang demonstrates the crucial role of private enterprise in rural China in the 1980s that spurred the tremendous economic growth that lifted hundreds of millions out of poverty. These "peasant entrepreneurs"—not Maoist revolutionaries—were the true authors of China's "Great Leap Forward." Huang also makes a compelling analytical case that the reactionary crackdown in China in the 1990s after Tiananmen Square—wherein the Communist Party, its 46 million government bureaucrats, state-owned enterprises, and the People's Liberation Army reasserted state capitalism from their power bases in China's coastal cities—has all but crushed the rural sector.

Of particular relevance is Huang's illustration of the statists' de facto mandatory, "Chinese-style" CSR imposed by the regime only on the truly *private* Chinese companies. These companies could become "glorious" in the eyes of the state only by making social contributions "in the form of charity and donations to poverty alleviation and reforestation."

Though CSR advocates routinely blame the Reagan–Thatcher era of deregulation for any number of consequences that now require CSR-style solutions, regulation continues to grow worldwide. In the United States, regulation has grown dramatically in recent decades, as evidenced by the expanding number of pages in the Code of Federal Regulations (CFR): In 2009, the CFR expanded by about 25 percent—from 132,228 pages in 1993 to 163,333 pages. In addition, the Obama Administration's regulatory wave, especially in the areas of health care, energy, and finance, provides further evidence that the regulatory state is alive and well.

Evidence of this more radical version of CSR can be found in many international documents laying out its principles and policies over the past two years:

- December 2010: ISO 26000 International Standard: Guidance on Social Responsibility;

- January 2011: U.N. Global Compact, Blueprint for Corporate Sustainability Leadership;

- March 2011: Global Reporting Initiative, Sustainability Reporting Guidelines, Version G3.1;

- May 2011: OECD Guidelines for Multinational Enterprises, Amendments Relating to National Contact Points;

- June 2011: United Nations Guiding Principles for Business and Human Rights; and

- October 2011: European Union Commission's Renewed Strategy 2011–14 for Corporate Social Responsibility.

Indeed, ISO 26000 is one of the most comprehensive expressions of the new CSR agenda to date. It claims to have achieved "international consensus" on the topic.

Comprehensive CSR Rights and Duties

ISO 26000 is the first CSR standard to attempt a comprehensive delineation of CSR principles, and it does so in more than 100 pages of text. The key to understanding the comprehensive nature of ISO 26000 principles is the term "international norms of behavior," which is defined by ISO 26000 as "expectations of socially responsible behaviour derived from customary international law, generally accepted principles of international law, or intergovernmental agreements that are universally or nearly universally recognized." The expansive scope of the definition of "international norms of behaviour" is fully revealed only when companies understand that this term:

- takes principles which are only directly applicable to governments and extends them to business;

- encompasses not just international law, but an array of other "intergovernmental" agreements;

- extends the application of all norms to all countries; even if a country has not signed a treaty or other "intergovernmental agreement," as long as "nearly" all countries have, then the norm becomes applicable in all countries;

- is further expanded by the opening phrase "expectations of socially responsible behavior derived from"—

international norms of behavior are not actually found in the designated sources, but are "derived from" those sources; and

- is applied not only to a company's operations and activities but also to any other organization within the company's "sphere of influence."

Earlier drafts of ISO 26000 had a narrower definition of "international norms of behaviour." Working Draft 4.2, for instance, defined International Norms of Behaviour as "norms that are universally, or nearly universally recognized, and based on customary international law, generally accepted principles of international law, or authoritative intergovernmental instruments." Section 4.7 of that Working Draft reinforced this definition by emphasizing that international norms are principles "that are based on or derived from customary international law, generally accepted principles of international law, or from sources of public international law such as treaties." However, in the latter stages of the ISO 26000 drafting process, a much broader range of sources was accepted to transform ISO 26000's definition of norms into an "NGO wish list" of environmental and social obligations in the name of societal demand.

A "Wish List"

In fact, ISO 26000 cites over 60 of the United Nation's International Labour Organization (ILO) conventions, recommendations, codes, and guidelines as well as over 40 other U.N. treaties, reports, and declarations, all apparently constituting ISO 26000's sources of "international norms of behavior." Among them is an array of treaties and conventions which the U.S. has not ratified, including:

- The U.N. Convention on Biological Diversity;

- The Kyoto Protocol to the U.N. Framework Convention on Climate Change;

- The U.N. International Covenant on Economic, Social, and Cultural Rights;

- The Second Optional Protocol to the International Convention on Civil and Political Rights, aiming at the abolition of the death penalty;

- The ILO Termination of Employment Convention, 1982;

- The ILO Part-Time Work Convention, 1994;

- The ILO Paid Educational Leave Convention, 1974; and

- The ILO Workers with Family Responsibilities Convention, 1981.

Moreover, ISO 26000 freely employs aspirational principles in its effort to manufacture a foundation for corporate social responsibility, including references to the Rio Declaration on Environment and Development, the U.N. Millennium Declaration, and the ILO Declaration on Social Justice for a Fair Globalization.

The breadth and depth of the resulting "wish list" is truly astonishing. While Clause 4 of ISO 26000 summarizes the "Principles of Social Responsibility" in a relatively modest four pages, Clause 6 details the criteria for these principles of social responsibility—in 50 pages of text. These 50 pages subject businesses to comprehensive standards relating to

- employment practices,

- the environment,

- fair operating principles,

- human rights,

- consumer issues, and

- community involvement and development.

- This comprehensive statement of international norms of behavior, includes a number of controversial standards:

- The precautionary approach to environmental issues;

- The preparation of an environmental impact statement before engaging in new product development or any action affecting the environment;

- Recognition of human-induced climate change and a commitment to actions to remedy that change;

- In employment law, adoption of comparable worth and rejection of the employment-at-will doctrine;

- Disclosure of political contributions; and

- Achieving gender parity in the company's "governing structure and management."

Not only is the description of norms comprehensive, but the obligation of companies is weighted towards conformity with the entire standard: The ability of companies to choose particular areas of "doing good" is limited by the fact that the final text of ISO 26000 *eliminated* the only criteria in its section on "Determining Significance" that would have specifically recognized that firms could weigh the costs of taking action on principles of social responsibility. Earlier drafts of the ISO 26000 standard, up to and including the "Draft International Standard" text released in June 2009, specifically recognized that firms could consider at least in part the "potential effect of the related action compared to the resources required for implementation." However, the Final Draft International Standard, which became the official text of ISO 26000 in December 2010, eliminated the phrase "compared to the resources required for implementation." The final wording of the clause states only that companies should consider the "potential effect of taking action or failing to take action on the issue." Companies will clearly be at a disadvantage under that standard, as the potential effect of failing to take action on education, health, environment, or any other topic could be said to outweigh the company's own concerns.

Undefined Expectations

ISO 26000's definition of norms of behavior is also troubling because it ties the concept of norms to undefined "expectations," and therefore to no definitive standard at all. The definition begins with the phrase "expectations of socially responsible conduct derived from" and then recites the wide array of designated norms identified above. It is unclear how the "expectations" are to be "derived," but, ultimately, ISO 26000 ties "expectations" back to the concept of sustainable development as a whole: "Because sustainable development is about the economic, social and environmental goals common to all people, it can be used as a way of summing up the broader expectations of society that need to be taken into account by organizations seeking to act responsibly." Thus, it would appear that a norm can exist if it is deemed important for sustainable development, even if the norm is not found in any existing document.

Extending Obligations

Finally, the new CSR seeks to extend obligations beyond the individual company to countries where it does business and other companies with which it does business. Companies have both a "sphere of influence" on others, and must avoid "complicity" in violations of the standards by others. The sphere of influence can extend to any supplier or customer with which a company does business. Complicity means that a company may also have an obligation to make sure that any country in which it does business meets all standards—including on education, health care, and environment—or shut down its business in that country.

The International Organization for Standardization

The ISO story began in 1946 when delegates from 25 countries met at the Institute of Civil Engineers in London and decided to create a new international organization "to facilitate the international coordination and unification of industrial standards." In February 1947 the new organisation, ISO, officially began operations.

Since then, we have published over 19,500 International Standards covering almost all aspects of technology and manufacturing.

Today we have members from 164 countries and 3 368 technical bodies to take care of standard development. More than 150 people work full time for ISO's Central Secretariat in Geneva, Switzerland.

International Organization for Standardization,
"Our Story," www.iso.org, 2013.

ISO 26000 also provides no indication of how small and medium-size companies are to meet these obligations. ISO 26000 does specifically assure small and medium-sized companies that 100 pages of standards can mean that "[i]ntegrating social responsibility throughout the SMO can be undertaken through practical, simple and cost efficient actions, and does not need to be complex or expensive." ISO 26000 contains only one reference to company size: When the company studies how it should integrate social responsibility "throughout its organization," ISO 26000 states that the review should include "the organization's type, purpose, nature of operations and size." However, even that one reference is seemingly negated by sub-clause 7.3.2.1 on "determining relevance" of issues to be addressed by the company, as that section does not allow companies to take into account cost or company size.

The "NORMAPME User Guide for European SMEs on ISO 26000" developed by the EU-funded European Office of Crafts, Trades and Small and Medium-sized Enterprises for Standardisation (NORMAPME) states that the guide "intends to lend support to the efficient use of ISO 26000 by European small and medium-sized enterprises." However, the User Guide cites no specific language from ISO 26000 as the basis for such "efficient use." Indeed, it could not cite that language because it is not there. Is the User Guide consistent with ISO 26000? It is a possible interpretation—but by no means clearly reflected in the text of ISO 26000.

Reject the ISO 26000

Activists for statist intervention in private free enterprise have been steadily ramping up their push for more corporate social responsibility (CSR) both in the U.S. and globally. Deploying their "doing well by doing good" mantra they have succeeded in enshrining CSR principles not only through the International Organization for Standardization's "ISO 26000 International Standard: Guidance on Social Responsibility," but also with such vehicles as the Organization for Economic Cooperation and Development's Stakeholder Advisory Board for the OECD Guidelines for Multinational Enterprises and the U.N. Global Compact.

While the language sounds innocuous enough—to "promote awareness . . . work with governments, foreign businesses, international labor and civil society organizations . . . and offer a forum for confidential discussion between business and stakeholders," this latest and more radical phase of CSR is more intrusive and changes the focus from voluntary initiatives to mandated standards, from targeted projects to comprehensive obligations, from flexible communications to highly structured reporting.

As Jim Kelly of the Federalist Society and Global Governance Watch points out, these groups are seeking to use a

> matrix of human rights governance networks to bypass national courts, democracy, and the rule of law to develop 'soft law' human rights norms, with which multinational business enterprises will have to comply from the early stages of project research, design, and planning through project completion and beyond.

The definition of CSR has increasingly cast aside the traditional responsibility of company management to the firm's owners and has instead coalesced around the claim of a triple-bottom-line obligation of companies to deliver economic, social, and environmental "returns" to justify what the left calls the license to operate. In the CSR world, private companies that operate in these markets become "responsible" only by meeting codes such as ISO 26000. This completely ignores the fundamental benefits that companies provide to society through the goods and services they supply, the jobs they generate, and the economic freedom that results.

If the governments and business communities of developed countries fail to resist and block this wave of more radical CSR now, there is a real danger that its proponents will push the new CSR beyond the point of no return.

Periodical and Internet Sources Bibliography

The following articles have been selected to supplement the diverse views presented in this chapter.

The Economist	"Good Business; Nice Beaches," May 19, 2012.
Nancy Folbre	"The Profits of Virtue," *New York Times*, April 9, 2012.
Adrian Henriques	"What Are Standards For? The Case of ISO 2600," *The Guardian*, January 5, 2012.
Greg Hewitt	"Corporate Social Responsibility Goes Beyond Just Signing on the Dotted Line," *The Huffington Post*, October 3, 2013.
Paul Klein	"Is CSR As We Know It Obsolete?" *Forbes*, October 29, 2012.
Knowledge@Wharton	"Does the Good Outweigh the Bad? Sizing Up 'Selective' Corporate Social Responsibility," June 5, 2013.
Ben Lewis	"Corporate Social Enterprise Needs Time and Resources," *The Guardian*, August 14, 2013.
Steve Lohr	"First, Make Money. Also, Do Good," *New York Times*, August 13, 2011.
Aarti Maharaj	"Can Corporate Social Responsibility Really Matter? Really?" *Corporate Secretary*, January 18, 2011.
Kasper Nielson	"Is CSR Dead? Or Just Mismanaged?" *Forbes*, December 11, 2012.
Irving Wladawsky-Berger	"Reshaping Business and Capitalism for the 21st Century," *Wall Street Journal*, October 11, 2013.

OPPOSING
VIEWPOINTS®
SERIES

CHAPTER 2

What Is the Goal of an Effective Corporate Social Responsibility Strategy?

Chapter Preface

On November 10, 1995, a group of nine Nigerian activists were executed by the Nigerian military government after months of illegal detention, brutal torture, and a sham trial. The nine activists, known as the Ogoni Nine, were members of the Movement for the Survival of the Ogoni People (MOSOP), a nonviolent organization protesting the exploitation of the Ogoni by large oil companies in the Niger Delta, an oil-rich region in southern Nigeria. For years, MOSOP had opposed the environmental degradation of the land by the multinational Royal Dutch Shell Group. Under the leadership of environmental activist and writer Ken Saro-Wiwa, MOSOP became more successful in its attempts to bring worldwide awareness to the deteriorating environmental and human rights situation in the region. The group petitioned the corrupt military government, led by the ruthless General Sani Abacha, for environmental protections and an end to a series of human rights abuses in the Niger Delta.

In the summer of 1994, Saro-Wiwa and eight other MOSOP leaders were detained illegally on bogus murder charges, held in military custody without legal representation, tortured repeatedly, and then convicted and sentenced to death by a military tribunal. While awaiting trial, Saro-Wiwa reflected on the fight to make the world a better place. "Whether I live or die is immaterial," he wrote from his cell. "It is enough to know that there are people who commit time and energy to fight this one evil among so many others predominating worldwide. If they do not succeed today, they will succeed tomorrow. We must keep on striving to make the world a better place for all of mankind—each one contributing his bit, in his or her own way."[1]

Just ten days after the Ogoni Nine were convicted, they were executed by the military government.

In 1996 the families of the Ogoni Nine, as well as members of MOSOP and other human rights activists in Nigeria who had been imprisoned and tortured by the military government, began to seek justice against the Nigerian government and Royal Dutch Shell for their shameful role in the Ogoni Nine injustice.

In 2002 twelve Nigerian citizens filed a complaint against Royal Dutch Shell and Shell Transport and Trading Company in the Southern District of New York alleging that the oil companies aided and abetted violations of human rights law. The plaintiffs in the lawsuit included the wife of the late Dr. Barinem Kiobel, one of the Ogoni Nine.

The plaintiffs justified bringing the case in front of a US court by citing the Alien Tort Statute (ATS), a law enacted in 1789 that allows claims to be adjudicated in American courts when violations of international law involve US corporations, or multinational corporations with business in the United States. Under the ATS, a number of egregious crimes—slave labor, sex trafficking, torture—that have been sanctioned by large corporations have been heard in US courts.

However, in 2013 the US Supreme Court held that *Kiobel v. Royal Dutch Shell* should be dismissed, citing that the ATS was not applicable to the case. In his opinion, Chief Justice John Roberts wrote that the ATS should have a very limited scope, especially when applied to violations occurring outside of the United States.

The *Kiobel* case illuminated the international debate over the responsibility corporations should have for the protection of human rights around the globe. Human rights is one of the topics discussed in the following chapter, which examines several elements of a successful corporate social responsibility strategy. Other viewpoints in the chapter explore the importance of corporations focusing on environmental and human sustainability, fighting poverty, and building social institutions.

Note

1. Karen McGregor, "Ogoni Nine Hanged as Indifferent West Failed to Respond," *The Independent*, September 19, 2000. www.independent.co.uk.

> *"In its original and broadest sense, sustainability is about longevity—the capacity to survive and prosper over generations."*

Corporations Should Embrace Sustainability as a Strategy

Dan Gray

Dan Gray is an author and the visiting fellow of the Ashridge Centre for Business and Sustainability. In the following viewpoint, he advocates sustainability as a business strategy, contending that it is about longevity and fundamental long-term business viability. Gray suggests that sustainability is more than just being "green," it should be the cornerstone of a corporate value system that recognizes the link between long-term success and serving a higher social purpose. For many businesses, he says, that has meant a reevaluation of purpose and mission—and a strategic branding that results in market success.

As you read, consider the following questions:

1. Who does Gray identify as one of the great pioneers of sustainable business?

2. To what does the term "thicker value" refer?

3. According to Gray, how did Field Marshal Helmuth von Moltke define strategy?

"Once you see, you can't unsee," was apparently a be-loved phrase of one of my heroes—the sadly departed Ray C. Anderson, founder of Interface and one of the great pioneers of sustainable business.

If you're reading this as one who 'sees', whatever your own personal epiphany about sustainability, I'll warrant you've never looked at the world in quite the same way since. But it can be very easy to forget/ignore how we saw the world before our own paradigm shifted, and to judge others who haven't yet experienced it. Even when our beliefs change, we have an amazing capacity as humans to convince ourselves that we've held them all along.

We should instead also make a point of exploring different ways to put the case for sustainability to the sceptical congregation—starting with the (possibly heretical) assertion that it's got nothing to do with being green.

When we allow sustainability to be defined largely or exclusively in terms of the word 'green', we cut off the blood supply to a much broader and richer narrative.

In its original and broadest sense, sustainability is about longevity—the capacity to survive and prosper over generations. Framing it as such provides much more fertile territory for meaningful discussion with sceptical business leaders, because it poses infinitely bigger and more relevant questions (to them) about fundamental long-term business viability.

Business must now operate within a completely different set of conditions, encompassing the combined forces not only of climate change, population growth and diminishing natural resources, but also (among others) the ascent of Generation Y and increased public scrutiny in the wake of the financial crisis.

To achieve longevity, they will need to recognise these seismic shifts and re-imagine them, not as constraints on business as usual, but as the perfect opportunity to reconnect with disillusioned customers and employees by designing something better. It's worth noting the words with which Unilever chief executive Paul Polman launched their Sustainable Living Plan, "not as a project to celebrate, but a new business model to implement."

Those that 'see' understand that sustainability isn't a discrete agenda. It's a cultural thing—a perspective on core business strategy that inextricably links long-term success with serving a higher social purpose.

Putting Purpose at the Heart of Profit

It is probably unlikely that most business leaders would turn to a creative agency to advise their business on corporate strategy. But maybe they should.

That's because, more than ever before, the business that wants to achieve long-term success must earth itself in a sure sense of why it exists, what it stands for, and why it matters. And that purpose should be self-evident in the very products and services it provides, how it organises itself, and how it conducts its daily business—this is strategic branding.

Brand is what ultimately connects the success stories behind companies as diverse as young upstarts, like Innocent and Icebreaker, to established giants, like Interface, Unilever and Marks & Spencer.

In their own ways, what all these organisations have done is to put an enduring sense of purpose at the heart of their core business strategy—a reason for being that unites the beliefs of people inside the business with the fundamental human values of the people the business serves.

Why do you exist (beyond making money for shareholders)? Why should people choose to buy from you?

Sustainability

At its broadest level, environmental or global sustainability refers to Earth's ability to continue functioning in a manner that supports humans and other ecosystems. Sustainability includes a host of environmental, economic, and social issues. It is common to hear about sustainable agriculture, business, development, education, lifestyles, policies, and sustainability science. The United Nations Division for Sustainable Development lists more than forty different issues of current concern relating to sustainability, including atmosphere, climate change, demographics (population growth and structure), energy, international law, poverty, sanitation, and toxic chemicals.

Proponents of sustainability practices often promote three primary targets—the control of population growth; the adequate distribution, use, and care of resources; and changing patterns of consumption—as facets of developing and promoting sustainable ways of life.

"Sustainability," Global Issues in Context Online Collection, *2013.*

Why should they drag themselves out of bed in the morning to come and work for you? If you ceased to exist tomorrow, why should anyone miss you?

In a world of increasingly rapid change, only authentic and compelling answers to these kinds of questions provide the means to achieve long-term success. Business models will inevitably come and go. What can and should unite them all, however, is an overarching preoccupation with delivering what Umair Haque refers to as thicker value—the reconnection of business strategy to social progress.

Out With the New, in With the Old

If the idea of entrusting corporate strategy to a bunch of creative types puts the fear of god into you—rest assured that this whole thesis is grounded in long-established (though apparently also long-forgotten) principles of successful strategy formulation.

Field Marshal Helmuth von Moltke defined strategy in 1871 as "a system of expedients . . . the evolution of an original guiding idea under constantly changing circumstances." It seems tailor-made for these times.

So the question isn't whether you can afford to use the creative experts to find your purpose, it's whether you can afford not to. Like it or not, purpose is the beating heart of your business. And if you can't feel its pulse, then your business may find itself heading for the morgue.

> *"The good news is that consumers are taking the first step in combating industrial greenwashing practices worldwide by becoming more critical of industry rhetoric."*

Corporate Environmental Sustainability Claims Are Merely "Greenwashing"

Adam Kingsmith

Adam Kingsmith is an associate at the Public Intellectuals Project and a contributor to several periodicals, including The International. *In the following viewpoint, he contends that too many corporations are engaging in greenwashing—exaggerating environmental claims about their products and practices in order to garner positive public relations or to distract from the environmentally destructive aspects of their business. Kingsmith points out that as the media and the public's environmental awareness has grown, corporate public relations strategies have become even more sophisticated and deceptive. The proliferation of misleading green-marketing campaigns, he argues, has made it difficult for the consumer to differentiate from corporations truly committed to eco-friendly practices and those engaging in green-washing. The Internet has been a valuable tool in this regard, Kingsmith maintains, because it allows conscientious consumers to learn about products and corporations and take action against industrial greenwashing practices.*

As you read, consider the following questions:

1. According to Kingsmith, where does the term "greenwashing" originate?

2. What advertising tagline does Kingsmith identify as the one that won British Petroleum (BP) a gold medal from the American Marketing Association in 2000?

3. What bank has been deemed by Ethical Consumer to be one of the least ethical banks on the planet, according to the viewpoint?

"Green is the new black," proclaims Greenpeace International. "Corporations are falling all over themselves to demonstrate to current and potential customers that they are not only ecologically conscious, but also environmentally correct."

These newfound corporate environmental consciences are part of a phenomenon known as "greenwashing." The term originated from a 1986 essay by New York environmentalist Jay Westervelt which examined the hospitality industry's practice of asking guests to reuse their towels in order to "save the environment."

What's Behind Greenwashing?

Environmental lawyers Devika Kewalramani and Richard J. Sobelsohn of *Forbes Magazine* attribute the origins of greenwashing to an amalgamation of the "concepts of 'green' (to be environmentally sound), and 'whitewashing' (to gloss over wrongdoing) to describe the deceptive use of green marketing which promotes a misleading perception that a company's policies, practices, products or services are environmentally friendly."

What Greenpeace calls "the cynical use of [the] environmental theme to whitewash corporate misbehavior" first occurred long before Westervelt's label came about. However, as the media and the public's environmental awareness have grown, the sophistication of corporate public relation strategies has been forced to intensify in order to keep up.

"'Eco-friendly,' 'organic,' 'natural,' and 'green,'" elaborate Kewalramani and Sobelsohn of *Forbes*, "are just some everyday examples of widely used labels that can be confusing, even misleading." Such misrepresentations are increasing in scope and scale as organizations successfully portray themselves as environmental stewards because consumers have little information regarding corporate operations and practices.

There are of course some businesses who are genuine in their commitments to eco-friendly practices and policies. Nevertheless, too many others seem to be facetiously treating "environmentalism" like it is a tagline as opposed to a corporate commitment.

"Buy our products," mocks Greenpeace, "and you will end global warming, improve air quality, and save the oceans." At best, statements such as these stretch the truth, and at worst, they obscure environmentally harmful corporate behaviors.

Indoctrinating the Consumer

According to Dr. Tiffany Gallicano of the University of Oregon, "as more companies have adopted green marketing campaigns, consumers are growing increasingly confused over what it means to be 'green.'"

This makes it progressively more difficult for the consumer to differentiate between those companies authentically committed to greener practices and those using a green curtain to conceal more environmentally degrading motives.

As the commerce review *Brandweek* notes, even those corporations that are genuinely concerned with environmentally friendly practices are motivated first and foremost by revenue; "it's unlikely they'd be pursuing this angle if there weren't profit to be had."

Moreover, according to *The Guardian*'s environmental correspondent Lucy Aitken, "the companies that are making the biggest strides internally tend to be the most bashful in their communications, while those that are most vocal have the least to say." Thus, it seems that the fervency of a corporation's environmentalist claims and the truthfulness of those claims are inversely correlated.

When corporations do manage to voluntarily improve their green practices, they often use multi-million dollar publicity campaigns to advertise minor improvements as major achievements. Furthermore, as Greenpeace highlights, some disingenuous companies, "when forced by legislation or a court decision to improve their environmental track record, promote the resulting changes as if they had taken the step voluntarily."

"The rhetoric has to match the reality of what a company is doing to address sustainability issues, as opposed to tinkering around the edges, or communicating a red herring," World Wildlife Fund head of industry relations Dax Lovegrove told Aitken.

Some corporately greenwashed red herrings have spurred recent lawsuits. But *Forbes* believes these are only the beginning, "as more businesses jump on the green bandwagon, and rising public intolerance for false green claims is experienced, it is only a matter of time before there is a groundswell in court actions or other proceedings."

The Scope and Spread of Greenwashing

John Grant, co-founder of renowned UK advertising agency St. Lukes, writes in his *The Green Marketing Manifesto*, "you

'GREENWASHING' ALL TOO COMMON
A new study has found that nearly all "green" consumer products make a false, misleading or unproven environmental claim to attract eco-conscious shoppers...

© Aislin/CagleCartoons.com.

can't put a lettuce in the window of a butcher's shop and declare that you are now 'turning vegetarian.'"

Unfortunately, according to Guy Pearse, author of *Greenwash: Big Brands and Carbon Scams*, this is what many corporations are attempting to do: "Toyota reckons Mother Nature drives a Prius, Ford wants us to 'Join the Green Revolution', and McDonald's has painted its famous golden arches green. Facebook has even 'friended' Greenpeace."

The scale of this green branding swindle is colossal. In selling products to consumers who want to cut their carbon footprints, lots of companies advertise their offerings as emission-free cornerstones of an increasingly popular "save the planet" lifestyle.

An example of the greenwasher par excellence is energy multinational British Petroleum (BP). In 2000, BP won a Gold Medal from the American Marketing Association for adopting the tagline "beyond petroleum" and a Helios sunburst logo, pledging $8 billion to alternative energy, and promising to cut emissions to 10% below 1990 levels by 2010.

Unbeknownst at the time, these promises did not discuss the practical consequences of the company's 50,000 natural gas rigs and oil wells. Moreover, BP's latest figures indicate it produces 4 million barrels of oil daily, 24% more than when its "beyond petroleum" campaign started, adding about 1.7 million tonnes of CO_2 to the atmosphere daily.

BP claims its efficiency measures saved 7.9 million tonnes of CO_2 between 2002 and 2010, meaning emissions savings that took eight years to accumulate and promote are erased by BP's normal production every five days. Moreover, every 30 hours, BP wipes out all customer emissions savings made via offset programs over the last decade.

Besides BP and other titans of the energy sector such as Shell, Vale, Chevron, and Sasol, many other corporations engage [in] greenwashing practices that are becoming increasingly recognized by the critical consumer.

Asia Pulp and Paper (APP), a corporation that [has] done business with large conglomerates such as Mattel, Yum! (parent company of KFC, Pizza Hut, and Taco Bell), and Wal-Mart, has gone to extreme lengths to greenwash the deforestation of over 2 million hectares of Indonesian forests which are home to the endangered Sumatran tiger.

The agricultural giant and world's largest producer of genetically modified (GM) seeds Monsanto, greenwashes with their tagline of "producing more, conserving more," while in actuality, a 13-year independent US study determined that GM maize and soybeans produce yields no greater, and in many cases much lower, than conventional crops.

Banking multinational HSBC claims to be "respecting environmental limits and investing in communities." However, Ethical Consumer ranks HSBC as one of the least ethical banks on the planet due to its score of 2.5 out of 20 for continued investment in coal mining, tar sands extraction, offshore gas and oil drilling, and unsustainable logging.

Fighting Back Against Misinformation

The good news is that consumers are taking the first step in combating industrial greenwashing practices worldwide by becoming more critical of industry rhetoric. "Things are changing," said Greenpeace Canada's forest campaign coordinator and one of Canada's 2013 Clean 50 honorees Richard Brooks, "people are getting a lot smarter."

"Consumers are becoming increasingly aware of corporate social responsibility and are expecting more information and disclosure from companies," said Dr. Gallicano. "The information technology age has had a profound impact on the flow of information. The control of information resides with individuals rather than companies."

According to Greenpeace International, the Internet is an increasingly valuable medium through which consumers can take action against industrial greenwashing practices. Activist or not, consumers can contact corporations and policymakers to voice concerns or draw attention to misleading claims via blogs, websites, and other socio-digital forms of outreach.

A recent example of successful action against greenwashers was Greenpeace's Kleercut boycott of world-leading tissue-product manufacturer, the Kimberly-Clark Corporation.

In 2009, after 5 years of campaigning against the company's "green" claims, Greenpeace convinced Kimberly-Clark to stop buying pulp from endangered Canadian boreal forests, and instead ensure that 100 per cent of its purchases came from responsible sources.

According to Brooks, the Kleercut campaign showed that individuals in the marketplace do have significant influence over corporate behavior.

However, since Terrachoice, North America's premier environmental marketing firm, found that 98% of 2,219 products surveyed in the United States and Canada are guilty of greenwashing practices, it seems that the environmentally-minded consumer must remain ever-vigilant in order to see through continued corporate embellishment.

> *"Rather than viewing organizational processes as ways of extracting more economic value, great companies create frameworks that use societal value and human values as decision-making criteria."*

The Aim of Corporations Should Be to Build Social Institutions

Rosabeth Moss Kanter

Rosabeth Moss Kanter is an author, the Ernest L. Arbuckle Professor of Business Administration at Harvard Business School, and director of Harvard University's Advanced Leadership Initiative. In the following viewpoint, she maintains that the traditional belief that the only responsibility corporations have is to its shareholders is a narrow and outdated way to think about the role of business in society. Kanter suggests that great companies have embraced the concept that business is an intrinsic part of society and have a key role in building and strengthening social institutions. She argues that this way of thinking, known as institutional logic, is essential to a corporation's long-term vi-

ability. Corporate leaders need to use institutional logic as a guiding principle in research, analysis, education, and managerial decision making, Kanter concludes.

As you read, consider the following questions:

1. How many people does the Mahindra Group employ in 100 countries?

2. What idea did Kanter propose to Novartis CEO Daniel Vasella that became a huge success and an annual event at the company?

3. How did Procter & Gamble employees reduce the high rates of infant mortality in West Africa, according to Kanter?

It's time that beliefs and theories about business catch up with the way great companies operate and how they see their role in the world today. Traditionally, economists and financiers have argued that the sole purpose of business is to make money—the more the better. That conveniently narrow image, deeply embedded in the American capitalist system, molds the actions of most corporations, constraining them to focus on maximizing short-term profits and delivering returns to shareholders. Their decisions are expressed in financial terms.

I say convenient because this lopsided logic forces companies to blank out the fact that they command enormous resources that influence the world for better or worse and that their strategies shape the lives of the employees, partners, and consumers on whom they depend. Above all, the traditional view of business doesn't capture the way great companies think their way to success. Those firms believe that business is an intrinsic part of society, and they acknowledge that, like family, government, and religion, it has been one of society's pillars since the dawn of the industrial era. Great companies work to make money, of course, but in their choices of how to do so, they think about building enduring institutions. They invest in the future while being aware of the need to build people and society.

Today's Successful Companies

In this article, I turn the spotlight on this very different logic—a social or institutional logic—which lies behind the practices of many widely admired, high-performing, and enduring companies. In those firms, society and people are not afterthoughts or inputs to be used and discarded but are core to their purpose. My continuing field research on admired and financially successful companies in more than 20 countries on four continents is the basis for my thinking about the role of institutional logic in business.

Institutional logic holds that companies are more than instruments for generating money; they are also vehicles for accomplishing societal purposes and for providing meaningful livelihoods for those who work in them. According to this school of thought, the value that a company creates should be measured not just in terms of short-term profits or paychecks but also in terms of how it sustains the conditions that allow it to flourish overtime. These corporate leaders deliver more than just financial returns; they also build enduring institutions.

Rather than viewing organizational processes as ways of extracting more economic value, great companies create frameworks that use societal value and human values as decision-making criteria. They believe that corporations have a purpose and meet stakeholders' needs in many ways: by producing goods and services that improve the lives of users; by providing jobs and enhancing workers' quality of life; by developing a strong network of suppliers and business partners; and by ensuring financial viability, which provides resources for improvements, innovations, and returns to investors.

In developing an institutional perspective, corporate leaders internalize what economists have usually regarded as externalities and define a firm around its purpose and values. They undertake actions that produce societal value—whether or not those actions are tied to the core functions of making and selling goods and services. Whereas the aim of financial logic is to maximize the returns on capital, be it shareholder or owner value, the thrust of institutional logic is to balance public interest with financial returns.

Institutional logic should be aligned with economic logic but need not be subordinate to it. For example, all companies require capital to carry out business activities and sustain themselves. However, at great companies profit is not the sole end; rather, it is a way of ensuring that returns will continue. The institutional view of the firm is thus no more idealized than is the profit-maximizing view. Well-established practices, such as R&D and marketing, cannot be tied to profits in the short or long runs, yet analysts applaud them. If companies are to serve a purpose beyond their business portfolios, CEOs must expand their investments to include employee empowerment, emotional engagement, values-based leadership, and related societal contributions.

A New Approach

Business history provides numerous examples of industrialists who developed enduring corporations that also created social institutions. The Houghton family established Corning Glass and the town of Corning, New York, for instance. The Tata family established one of India's leading conglomerates and the steel city of Jamshedpur, Jharkhand. That style of corporate responsibility for society fell out of fashion as economic logic and shareholder capitalism came to dominate assumptions about business and corporations became detached from particular places. In today's global world, however, companies must think differently.

Globalization increases the speed of change; more competitors from more places produce surprises and shocks. An intensely competitive global economy places a high premium on innovation, which depends on human imagination, motivation, and collaboration. Global mergers and acquisitions add further complexity, with their success resting on how effectively the organizations are integrated. Moreover, seeking legitimacy or public approval by aligning corporate objectives with social values has become a business imperative. Corporations that cross borders face questions of cultural fit and local appropriateness; they must gain approval from governmental authorities, opinion leaders, and members of the public wherever they operate. Their employees are both internal actors and the company's representatives in the external community.

Only if leaders think of themselves as builders of social institutions can they master today's changes and challenges. I believe that institutional logic should take its place alongside economic or financial logic as a guiding principle in research, analysis, education, policy, and managerial decision making. . . .

A Common Purpose

Conceiving of the firm as a social institution serves as a buffer against uncertainty and change by providing corporations with a coherent identity.

As companies grow, acquire, and divest, the business mix changes frequently and job roles often vary across countries. So what exactly gives a company a coherent identity? Where are the sources of certainty that permit people to take action in an uncertain world? Purpose and values—not the widgets made—are at the core of an organization's identity, and they can guide people in their efforts to find new widgets that serve society.

Consider the Mahindra Group, an $11 billion multibusiness company based in Mumbai that employs 117,000 people in 100 countries. Like many emerging-market enterprises, the Mahindra Group operates in many industries, including automobiles, finance, IT, and several dozen others. And like the great companies, it invests in creating a culture based on a common purpose to provide coherence amidst diversity, proclaiming that it is "many companies united by a common purpose—to enable people to rise."

Performance with Purpose

Globalization detaches organizations from one specific society but at the same time requires that companies internalize the needs of many societies. Establishing clear institutional values can help resolve this complex issue. For example, PepsiCo has made health a big part of its aspiration to achieve Performance with Purpose. Nutrition, environmental responsibility, and talent retention are pillars supporting the slogan. Performance with Purpose provides strategic direction and motivation for diverse lines of business in many countries. It requires a gradual shift of resources from "fun for you" to "better for you" to "good for you," in PepsiCo parlance. It provides a rationale for acquisitions and investments. It is the logic behind the creation of a new organizational unit, the Global Nutrition Group, and new corporate roles, such as chief global health officer. It guides a quest to reduce or eliminate sugar and sodium in foods and beverages. Above all, it provides an identity for the people who work for PepsiCo all over the world.

Leaders can compensate for business uncertainty through institutional grounding. Great companies identify something larger than transactions or business portfolios to provide purpose and meaning. Meaning making is a central function of leaders, and purpose gives coherence to the organization. Institutional grounding involves efforts to build and reinforce organizational culture, but it is more than that. Culture is often a by-product of past actions, a passively generated outgrowth of history. Institutional grounding is an investment in activities and relationships that may not immediately create a direct road to business results but that reflect the values the institution stands for and how it will endure.

Institutional grounding can separate the survivors from those subsumed by global change. A sense of purpose infuses meaning into an organization, "institutionalizing" the company as a fixture in society and providing continuity between the past and the future. The name can change, but the identity and purpose will live on. In 2007, Spain's Grupo Santander acquired Brazil's Banco Real and folded it into its Brazilian assets. But Banco Real's spirit involved much more than its financial assets. Its then-CEO Fabio Barbosa was put in charge of creating the combined entity, Santander Brazil. Although the new organization faced pressure to increase branch profitability, under Barbosa's leadership Banco Real's focus on social and environmental responsibility, along with its private banking model, were infused throughout Santander Brazil and the parent.

Affirming Values and Purpose

Successful mergers are noteworthy for their emphasis on values and culture. When the merger of two Swiss pharmaceutical companies formed Novartis in 1996, CEO Daniel Vasella wanted the new company's mission to be globally meaningful and central to the integration and growth strategy. The question was how to provide employees with a tangible experience that reflected those values. When I floated the idea of a global day of community service—unheard of in Europe at that time—Novartis agreed. The company allowed each country organization to determine how it wanted to serve local communities, based on its interpretation of what the two histories and one future would suggest. The day of service has become an annual Novartis event, held on the merger's anniversary.

Affirming purpose and values through service is a regular part of how great companies express their identities. In June 2011, IBM celebrated its 100th anniversary by offering service to the world. Over 300,000 IBMers signed up to perform 2.6 million hours of service on a global service day. They contributed training and access to software tools, many of them developed specially for the occasion, to schools, governmental agencies, and NGOs. Projects included training on privacy and antibullying in 100 schools in Germany; a new website developed in India for the visually impaired, with a launch at 50 locations; and access to small-business resources for women entrepreneurs in the United States. The company gave the tools away, even in cases where the software could form the basis for commercial products, to demonstrate IBM's commitment to being a contributor to society.

A Long-Term Focus

Thinking of the firm as a social institution generates a long-term perspective that can justify any short-term financial sacrifices required to achieve the corporate purpose and to endure over time.

Keeping a company alive requires resources, so financial logic demands attention to the numbers. However, great companies are willing to sacrifice short-term financial opportunities if they are incompatible with institutional values. Those values guide matters central to the company's identity and reputation such as product quality, the nature of the customers served, and by-products of the manufacturing process. Banco Real, for instance, created a screening process to assess potential customers' societal standards as well as their financial standing. The bank was willing to walk away from those that did not meet its tests of environmental and social responsibility. This short-term sacrifice was prudent risk management for the longer term.

Companies using institutional logic are often willing to invest in the human side of the organization—investments that cannot be justified by immediate financial returns but that help create sustainable institutions. In South Korea, after the Asian financial crisis of the late 1990s, Shinhan Bank set out to acquire Chohung Bank, a larger and older bank that the government had bailed out. The moment the acquisition was announced, 3,500 male employees of a Chohung Bank union, whose ranks extended to management levels, shaved their heads in protest and piled the hair in front of Shinhan's headquarters in downtown Seoul. The acquirer then had to decide whether to go ahead with the acquisition and, if it did so, what it ought to do about Chohung's employees.

Shinhan's leaders applied institutional logic. They negotiated an agreement with the Chohung union, deferring formal integration for three years, giving equal representation to both Shinhan and Chohung managers on a new management committee, and increasing the salary of Chohung employees to match the higher wages of Shinhan employees. The acquirer also handed out 3,500 caps to cover the heads of the protestors. Shinhan invested heavily in what it called "emotional integration," holding a series of retreats and conferences intended not only to spread strategic and operational information but also to foster social bonding and a feeling of being "one bank." According to financial logic, the acquirer was wasting money. In terms of Shinhan's institutional logic, the investments were an essential part of securing the future.

The result: Within 18 months, Shinhan had grown both banks' customer bases, and the Chohung union was having a hard time fomenting discontent against the benign acquirer. Although a formal merger wouldn't occur for another year and a half, Shinhan and Chohung employees were working together on task forces and discussing best practices, and ideas were spreading that began to make the branches look more similar. Employees were, in essence, self-organizing. By the third year, when formal integration took place, Shinhan was outperforming not only the banking industry but also the South Korean stock market.

Emotional Engagement

The transmission of institutional values can evoke positive emotions, stimulate motivation, and propel self-regulation or peer regulation.

Utilitarian rationality is not the only force governing corporate performance and behavior inside organizations; emotions play a major role, too. Moods are contagious, and they can affect such issues as absenteeism, health, and levels of effort and energy. People influence one another, and in doing so they either increase or decrease others' performance levels, as my study of teams and organizations on winning and losing streaks reveals (see my book *Confidence*, Crown, 2004). Well-understood values and principles can be a source of emotional appeal, which can increase employee engagement. Having a statement of values has become common, so the issue is not whether a set of words called "values" exists somewhere in the company. Adhering to institutional logic makes the regular articulation of values core to the company's work. The CEOs of companies I studied, whether headquartered in the U.S., Mexico, the UK, India, or Japan, allocated considerable resources and their own time to breathing new life into long-standing values statements, engaging managers at many levels in the institutional task of communicating values. The point was not the words themselves but the process of nurturing a dialogue that would keep social purpose at the forefront of everyone's mind and ensure that employees use the organizational values as a guide for business decisions.

As a Procter & Gamble executive, Robert McDonald had long believed that the company's Purpose, Values, and Principles was a cornerstone of its culture, evoking strong emotions in employees and giving meaning to the company's brands. Within a month of becoming CEO in 2010, he elevated the purpose—improving the lives of the world's consumers—into a business strategy: improving more lives in more places more completely.

In P&G West Africa, for instance, every employee has a quantitatively measurable purpose-driven goal: How many more lives have I touched this year? So P&G West Africa's Baby Care Group set up Pampers mobile clinics to reduce high rates of infant mortality and help babies thrive. A physician and two nurses travel the region in a van, teaching postnatal care, examining babies, and referring mothers to hospitals for follow-ups or immunization shots. They also register mothers for mVillage, a text-message service (many of the poor in West Africa have cell phones) that offers health tips and the chance to ask questions of health care professionals. At the end of each mobile clinic visit, everyone gets two Pampers diapers. The emotional tugs for P&G employees are strong; they feel inspired by the fact that their product is at the center of a mission to save lives. They also feel proud that Pampers' sales have soared and that West Africa is among P&G's fastest-growing markets.

In companies that think of themselves as social institutions, work is emotionally compelling and meaning resides in the organization as a whole rather than in a less sustainable cult of personality. Top leaders exemplify and communicate the company's purpose and values, but everyone owns them, and the values become embedded in tasks, goals, and performance standards. Rather than depending on charismatic figures, great companies "routinize" charisma so that it spreads throughout the organization.

Partnering with the Public

The need to cross borders and sectors to tap new business opportunities must be accompanied by concern for public issues beyond the boundaries of the firm, requiring the formation of public-private partnerships in which executives consider societal interests along with their business interests.

One paradox of globalization is that it can increase the need for local connections. To thrive in diverse geographies and political jurisdictions, companies must build a base of relationships in each country with government officials and public intermediaries as well as suppliers and customers. Only by doing so can companies ensure that agendas are aligned even as circumstances—and public officials—keep changing. Those external stakeholders are interested as much in the corporations' contributions to the local community as they are in their transactional capabilities. At the same time, great companies want both an extended family of enduring relationships and a seat at the table on policy matters affecting their business.

Public-private partnerships to address societal needs are growing in number and importance, and are especially prevalent among enterprises that think institutionally. Partnerships can take many forms: International activities, conducted in collaboration with the United Nations and other global organizations (such as Procter & Gamble's Children's Safe Drinking Water program with UNICEF and several NGOs); large domestic projects, undertaken in collaboration with government ministries and development agencies (PepsiCo's agricultural projects in Mexico with the Inter-American Development Bank, for example); product or service development to address unmet societal needs (for instance, P&G's linkages with public hospitals in West Africa); or short-term volunteer efforts (IBM's work following the Asian tsunami, Hurricane Katrina, and earthquakes in China and Japan to provide software to track relief supplies and reunite families).

> *"There seems to be overwhelming evidence that organizational decisions have profound effects on employee physical and mental health and even people's life spans. Why, then does the human dimension of sustainability remain largely in the background?"*

Companies Emphasize the Environment over Employees

Jeffrey Pfeffer

Jeffrey Pfeffer is the Stanford Graduate School of Business Thomas Dee II Professor of Organizational Behavior. In the following viewpoint, he finds that while a growing number of companies have realized the importance of environmental sustainability, many do not prioritize human sustainability. Pfeffer asserts that organizational decisions that impact the lives and well-being of employees—health care, schedules, work environment, job security—should be of more concern to corporate officials. There have been studies, he points out, that suggest that human sustainability policies may pay off for companies, because happier and healthier employees are more productive and successful.

As you read, consider the following questions:

1. According to Pfeffer, what percent of Wal-Mart employees' children were either uninsured or on Medicaid in 2005?

2. According to a Harvard University study cited by Pfeffer, how many excess deaths per year in the United States can be attributed to a lack of health insurance?

3. What criteria does Pfeffer say are considered in the annual list of the best places to work, published by *Fortune* and the Great Places to Work Institute?

Eight years ago, Lee Scott, then CEO of Wal-Mart, made the first speech in the company's history broadcast to all of its associates. In that speech, Scott committed the company to the goals of being 100 percent supplied by renewable energy, creating zero waste, and selling products that sustain resources and the environment. Meanwhile, Wal-Mart paid its employees almost 15 percent less than other large retailers, and because of the lower pay, its employees made greater use of public health and welfare programs. In 2005, 46 percent of Wal-Mart employees' children were either uninsured or on Medicaid.

Wal-Mart's relative emphasis on the physical environment over its employees is far from unusual. British Petroleum, a company that touts its environmental credentials in its advertising and other presentations, was one of the first major oil companies to devote significant investment to alternative energy. Apparently less concerned about its people, the company paid a record fine of $87 million for an explosion in its Texas City, Texas, refinery that killed 15 workers.

Likewise, many other businesses have appointed "eco-managers" to oversee company efforts to become more energy-efficient and environmentally conscious, and companies track and publicly report carbon emissions from their activities. Yet one would be hard-pressed to find similar efforts focused on employees.

This lack of concern is puzzling given that health care costs, related in part to what companies do in the workplace, are an enormous problem in the United States and throughout the industrialized world. It is all the more surprising given the large epidemiological and public health literature that suggests there may be important organizational effects on human health and life span.

For example, in the United States, employer decisions about offering health insurance and the cost to employees, which can affect access, are consequential because there is a great deal of evidence showing that having health insurance affects health status. One study, by Andrew Wilper and his colleagues at Harvard University, estimated that there were more than 44,000 excess deaths per year in the United States because of lack of health insurance. Having health insurance also affects economic well-being. In 2005, Harvard's David U. Himmelstein and others published a study on a sample of personal-bankruptcy filers in five federal courts. About half the people filing for bankruptcy cited medical causes.

The relationship between other organizational behaviors and health are also widely established. Research shows that layoffs are very harmful to the physical and mental health of those laid off. It increases the likelihood that an individual will engage in violent behavior by some 600 percent, according to a study by Ralph Catalano at the University of California, Berkeley. A study of plant closings conducted in Sweden, a country with a relatively generous social safety net, found that mortality risk increased 44 percent in the four years following job loss. A New Zealand study reported that unemployed 25 to 64-year-olds had more than twice the odds of committing suicide. And downsizing is associated with negative changes in work behavior, increased smoking, less spousal support, and twice the rate of absence from work because of sickness.

Long hours also affect health. Haiou Yang, at the University of California, Irvine, found that compared with people who worked less than 40 hours a week, those who worked more than 51 hours were 29 percent more likely to report having hypertension, even after controlling for variables such as socioeconomic status, gender, age, diabetes, tobacco use, sedentary lifestyle, and body mass index. Long work hours also increase the likelihood that people will face a conflict between work and family responsibilities, which in turn is related to alcohol use, depression, and poor physical health, according to a 1996 study in the *Journal of Occupational Health Psychology*.

Job design also has important psychological consequences. High job demands that people cannot control, because they have little or no discretion over the pace and content of their work, coupled with work that is socially isolating, produce job stress. A series of studies of the British Civil Service showed that, even after controlling for numerous individual characteristics such as family background, serum cholesterol levels, blood pressure, and so forth, it was nevertheless the case that the higher someone's rank in the bureaucracy, the lower that person's risk of cardiovascular disease and death from heart attack.

Why the Physical Environment Takes Precedence Over Human Sustainability

There seems to be overwhelming evidence that organizational decisions have profound effects on employee physical and mental health and even people's life spans. Why, then does the human dimension of sustainability remain largely in the background? Why are polar bears, for instance, or even milk jugs

Top 3 Multinational Workplaces in 2012

1. SAS Institute

13,268 Employees

Industry: Information Technology

Employee Growth: 6.2%

Global Revenues: $2.7 billion

1st Year as a Great Place To Work: 1993

2. Google

34,311 Employees

Industry: Information Technology

Employee Growth: 19%

Global Revenues: $37.9 billion

1st Year as a Great Place To Work: 2006

3. NetApp

12,643 Employees

Industry: Information Technology/Data Management

Employee Growth: 7.6%

Global Revenues: $5.1 billion

1st Year as a Great Place To Work: 2008

Women in Senior Management: 23%

"The World's Best Multinational Workplaces,"
Great Place to Work Institute, 2013.

more important than people, not only in terms of research attention, but also as a focus of company initiatives?

One possibility is that the consequences of organizational actions on the physical environment are frequently much more visible. You can see the icebergs melting, polar bears stranded, forests cut down, and mountaintops reshaped by mining, and experience firsthand the dirty air and water that can come from company economic activities that impose externalities. Workers' reduced life expectancy and poorer physical and mental health status are more hidden from view. Even the occasional and well-publicized act of employee or exemployee violence has multiple causes and is often seen as aberrant behavior outside of the control and responsibility of the employer.

Another explanation is the differential actions taken to make sustainability salient. Organizations and groups focused on improving the physical environment have taken steps to increase the visibility of what companies do—reporting on carbon emissions and measures of environmental compliance, for instance, and trying to ensure that these reports generate news coverage.

Another factor that may explain the difference between environmental and human sustainability derives from the different actors in the two systems and the presumption of choice. Few would argue that trees choose to be cut down, that the air or water decides to be dirty, or that polar bears make decisions that result in the disappearance of food and habitat. Therefore, there is an implicit assumption that people must act on behalf of the environment because these entities can't act to affect their own interests. Employees, however, have choices, and exercise their choices in a labor market in which they compete for jobs and employers compete for talent. Presumably, if they don't like the conditions of their jobs, including the degree of inequality, the amount of stress, or the absence of health insurance, employees can decide to work elsewhere. At the limit, if the conditions of work are really life-threatening, employees can choose unemployment over ill health or premature death.

Does Human Sustainability Pay Off?

One of the major issues addressed by research on environmental sustainability has been whether adopting sustainability practices imposes net costs on companies, thereby eroding their competitiveness, or whether the benefits of being "green" more than outweigh any costs incurred.

Completely parallel questions and issues confront a focus on human sustainability. First, just as in the case of environmental pollution, companies that do not provide health insurance, lay people off, pay inadequate wages, and have work arrangements that stress their employees also impose externalities that others pay for even as they save on their own costs.

That's because some portion of the extra costs of increased illness fall on the broader health system through, for instance, increased use of public health and emergency room facilities. Second, just as green companies enjoy reputational benefits that help in brand building and product differentiation, so, too, we might expect that companies with better records of human sustainability could enjoy benefits in attracting and retaining employees and also in building a reputation that could attract additional consumer demand.

Indeed, there are some data that suggest that human sustainability may pay off for companies. Each year, the Great Place to Work Institute, in conjunction with *Fortune*, publishes lists of the best places to work. Most of the places are noted for their provision of good working conditions and benefits, including vacations, sick days, health insurance, training, and jobs that provide people with autonomy and challenge. The institute's website shows data indicating that companies on the "best companies" list consistently outperform benchmark indices over varying periods of time, indicating that, at least as measured by stock market performance, it is good to be a great place to work. How and why these returns accrue remains to be explored in more detail. But it is quite likely that, just as in the case of environmental sustainability, human sustainability pays.

Why is it so difficult to get companies to adopt practices consistent with human sustainability? After all, there is no reason why building sustainable companies should focus just on the physical and not the social environment. It is not just the natural world that is at risk from harmful business practices. We should care as much about people as we do about polar bears—or the environmental savings from using better milk jugs—and also understand the causes and consequences of how we focus our attention.

"Consumers in the United States still
buy products made by sweatshop workers, some of them trafficked, every
single day."

Corporations Should Ethically Produce Products and Not Exploit Workers

Jeff Ballinger

*Jeff Ballinger is an economic researcher and commentator and
expert on international labor issues. In the following viewpoint,
he states that proposed trade agreements with Colombia, Korea,
and Panama do not include adequate protections for labor, ensuring that widespread human trafficking and exploitation of
workers will continue in developing countries. At the heart of
this issue, he argues, is the refusal of US multinational corporations to act responsibly when it comes to producing their products. Global brands like Nike, Target, and Wal-Mart, Ballinger
maintains, outsource the manufacturing of cheap goods to sweatshops in developing countries; recent investigations have revealed
that many of these workers have been trafficked, underpaid,
overworked, exploited, and even abused. Corporate social responsibility (CSR) programs, according to Ballinger, have not*

prioritized the treatment of workers and need to do more. Consumers, strong unions, and independent factory monitors have been working to keep corporations accountable to ethical and responsible labor policies, he explains.

As you read, consider the following questions:

1. According to Ballinger, how much has the United States spent on programs to combat human trafficking since 2003?

2. How many employees does Ballinger estimate are on Nike's "responsibility" team?

3. According to the viewpoint, what was the amount of the settlement received by Cambodian textile workers in a suit brought against the owners of the garment company by the Worker Rights Consortium after a 2011 fire?

It's a cruel joke that Democratic politicians are trotting out language about "labor standards" to defend imminent trade agreements with Colombia, Korea, and Panama.

President Barack Obama sent Congress all three deals Monday [October 3, 2011], and lawmakers are expected to move quickly to approve them before the Korean president arrives October 13.

If legislators OK the deals as they stand, they will have learned nothing from previous trade pacts. Just look at the labor rights requirements in the 2001 U.S.-Jordan Free Trade Agreement.

These "protections" include boilerplate "core labor standards" on non-discrimination and rights to organize and bargain.

The stalwart anti-sweatshop team of Charlie Kernaghan and Barbara Briggs at the Institute for Global Labor and Human Rights uncovered a different story on the ground.

They reported last year [2010] that in one Jordanian factory, 1,200 guestworkers from Sri Lanka, Bangladesh, and India—75 percent of them women—had been trafficked, stripped of their passports, and held under conditions of indentured servitude.

Workers had been cheated of their promised wages, earning an average of just 35 cents an hour. The minimum wage in Jordan is 74.5 cents. The women were paid, at most, just $35.77 a week. The "labor rights" protections of that trade agreement proved an empty promise.

Under the Radar

Why are the garment factories in the Middle East kingdom of Jordan filled with Asians, when Jordan's unemployment rate is 30 percent?

The answer, as in so many countries, is that the factories that supply the global brands like Nike, Target, and Walmart can pay foreign workers less and—being "guests"—they are less likely to make trouble. Those that do make trouble are given the boot.

The Jordanian workers are not alone. All over the world, guestworkers toil far from their homes, often in conditions that resemble indentured servitude.

The issue of workers transported abroad has remained below the radar for years.

Throughout the last decade, a "perfect storm" developed: lucrative fees to brokers for delivering workers (often triple what laws allowed); growing demand for workers and relative impunity for brokers; bigger profits and malleable "host" governments; and complacency on the part of the buyers, the brands.

Sometimes guestworkers are unwilling guests. Trafficking—defined as workers being duped or sent against their will into jobs abroad—has exploded around the world as globalization has made national boundaries far more permeable and changes in the global financial system have made illicit money transfers far easier.

The United States has spent more than $800 million on programs to combat trafficking since 2003—to little effect.

California is trying to fight trafficking through a sunshine law. The shoe, apparel, toys, and electronics giants will have to cook up something new to comply with a new state law coming into effect January 1 [2012] that insists they report on trafficked workers in their supply chains.

Don't get your hopes up: Nike's feckless "responsibility" team—now numbering at least 210 employees—still goes around lamenting the fact that Nike HQ is powerless to control its suppliers.

For example, this year was the target date the company had set for ending forced overtime at supplier factories. Promises are easy to make, especially when no one's going to hold you to it.

Responsible for Nothing

So consumers in the United States still buy products made by sweatshop workers, some of them trafficked, every single day. Since U.S.-based brands are the mainstay buyers for these factories, why are Americans not better informed about workers' conditions?

The brands are complacent partly because they can easily deny that that they buy from sweatshops. All they have to do is adopt a simple code of conduct for supplier factories, promising to respect workers' rights.

Enforcement is a matter of "social audits," with inspections often announced ahead of time. The standard is often "follow local laws," which are weak.

But dozens of these global brands tout their "social responsibility" and publish extensive (if not particularly informative) "factory social audits" on their corporate websites.

Most Consumers Prefer That Corporations Change Operations

The one *approach to addressing social and environmental issues that consumers would like to see companies take:*

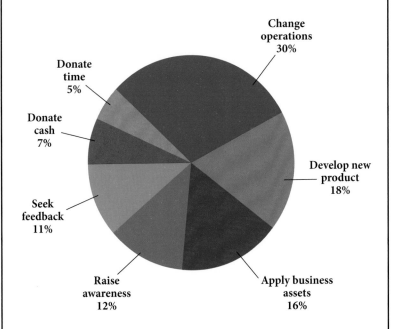

Change operations 30%

Donate time 5%

Donate cash 7%

Seek feedback 11%

Develop new product 18%

Raise awareness 12%

Apply business assets 16%

■ Change the way they operate, for example sourcing materials more responsibly or reducing the environmental impact of their factories.

■ Develop a new product or service (or enhance an existing one) that can help solve a social issue or is less harmful to the environment.

■ Apply their unique business assets, such as technology and research, to speed solutions to social and environmental problems.

■ Raise awareness for an issue and educate their consumers and employees.

■ Seek feedback from or develop partnerships with key stakeholders around social and environmental issues, for example with government agencies, nonprofits or other companies.

■ Make donations in the form of cash or products/services.

■ Donate the time and expertise of their employees.

TAKEN FROM: 2013 Cone Communications/Echo Global CSR Study.

Corporate Social Responsibility

"Corporate social responsibility" (CSR) programs adopted by corporations that source globally have exploded. The daily "CSRwire" compilation of press releases from corporate CSR offices shows 1,391 releases in one seven-month period last year.

But not one communiqué dealt with the issue of substandard wages, even though huge fights over wages are boiling throughout the apparel-producing world.

Tens of thousands of workers in Bangladesh and Cambodia protested and struck repeatedly last year over expected adjustments to the national minimum wage delayed for years—and which made pathetically little headway toward a "living" wage when it arrived in Bangladesh.

The unrest continues, despite repressive government intervention. A massive strike involving tens of thousands roiled a huge factory producing for Adidas in Vietnam earlier this year. The workers demanded an end to low wages and an unfair bonus system.

An Australia-based monitoring group feared for the strike leaders: Last year three young Vietnamese activists were handed prison sentences of seven to nine years for their involvement in a shoe-factory strike.

What to Do?

What can U.S. unions—and consumers—do to fight trafficking and the abysmal workplace conditions it creates?

We could learn a few lessons from anti-sweatshop campaigners. Even in the midst of a global economic downturn, diligent research by U.S. anti-sweatshop groups combined with determined activism on the part of wronged workers in Cambodia brought a measure of justice.

After a factory fire in March caused a textile company to close, the company refused to pay 4,000 workers the $600 to $700 in legally required severance they were owed. (None were injured in the blaze.)

While Cambodian workers marched on the boss en masse, the Worker Rights Consortium [WRC], a factory monitoring group established by anti-sweatshop campaigners, pressured Under Armour and Russell Athletic.

They were two of the brands that purchased the factory's goods. The WRC brought in the International Labor Organization and other international bodies, and before long the supplier was forced to follow the law—producing a $2.4 million settlement.

The WRC called it "the largest case so far in which labor rights monitoring efforts have succeeded in overcoming an attempt by garment factory owners to evade payment of legally owed compensation to workers."

We know that including labor rights language in trade deals hasn't stopped global corporations from exploiting workers and whitewashing their records with "social responsibility" baloney. So what can? Strong unions, pressure groups of consumers, and truly independent factory monitors are an imperfect—but far better—combination to hold them accountable.

> *"Companies are expected to be able to track the carbon footprint not only of their own manufacturing activities, but also their transportation, distribution and procurement activities, while monitoring the related activities of their extended supply chains as well."*

Corporations Should Practice Triple Bottom Line Reporting

Dave Blanchard

Dave Blanchard is a senior editor at Industry Week *and the author of* Supply Chain Management Best Practices. *In the following viewpoint, he contends that corporations should practice triple bottom line reporting, also known as corporate social responsibility (CSR) reporting. Triple bottom line, he explains, gives equal importance to labor, environmental, and financial disclosure in order to give the media and consumers an informed look at a company's sustainability initiatives and how it chooses to treat people and the planet in relationship to profits. Blanchard suggests that incomplete reporting can trigger a backlash and stakeholders will hold a company accountable for its failure*

Dave Blanchard, "Corporate Social Responsibility in the Supply Chain," *Industry Week*, May 14, 2012. This article originally appeared in the May 2012 edition of *Industry Week*, a Penton publication, and is used with permission. All rights reserved.

to practice the triple bottom line. For example, he says, Apple recently experienced some negative press for failing to fully disclose information on its carbon emissions and its monitoring of its global suppliers.

As you read, consider the following questions:

1. According to Blanchard, corporate social responsibility (CSR) or triple bottom line reporting has increased by how much from 2007 to 2011?

2. What is the Carbon Disclosure Project (CDP)?

3. What is Unilever's new goal regarding its purchase of palm oil, as cited by Blanchard?

Manufacturers are expected to fully disclose where they source their products, or suffer the PR backlash. Just ask Apple.

Corporate social responsibility (CSR) reporting, sometimes referred to as the triple bottom line (for "people, planet and profit"), has seen significant growth in the past five years, nearly tripling from 2,000 in 2007 to almost 6,000 in 2011, according to Corporate Register. Manufacturers in particular have taken to releasing these reports, if for no other reason than to keep their customers happy or at least informed about the nature of their sustainability initiatives.

An entire cottage industry of auditors and consultants has emerged to advise manufacturers on the numerous regulatory efforts in place or on the horizon, and virtually every industry sector has its own "green" initiatives and causes (e.g., free range, conflict-free minerals, Fairtrade, LEED, etc.). Companies are expected to be able to track the carbon footprint not only of their own manufacturing activities, but also their transportation, distribution and procurement activities, while monitoring the related activities of their extended supply chains as well. They're also expected to adhere to diversity and inclusion in their hiring practices.

That's not to say, of course, that all CSR reports are created equal, especially when it comes to nailing down exactly how a manufacturer reports its CSR activities. Companies that excel in the third P of the triple bottom line—profit—tend to be rewarded by Wall Street even if they come up a bit short on the people and planet side. However, such is the momentum toward full disclosure that even the biggest and most successful companies are being held accountable by stakeholders for incomplete reporting.

Apple, Inc.

The poster child for how not to reveal CSR activities is high-tech giant Apple Inc. Despite a well-deserved reputation for supply chain excellence, Apple has come up short in recent months due to its reluctance to fully disclose how it measures its carbon emissions and how it monitors the activities of its global suppliers. Apple, for instance, declined to participate in the Carbon Disclosure Project (CDP), an independent global system for companies to measure, disclose, manage and share climate change and water information. While more than 3,700 companies worldwide participate in the CDP, Apple does not (making it the largest IT company in the world to not participate). Having cultivated a cachet with the counterculture for decades, Apple's nondisclosure was viewed as a thumb in the eye to many of its adherents, especially after *The New York Times* criticized the company for effectively turning a blind eye toward the substandard labor practices of Foxconn, a Taiwan-based electronics manufacturer that assembles many of Apple's most popular products (iPads, iPhones, iPods, etc.).

Compounding matters, when Apple produced a 2012 progress report on its supplier responsibility, the company revealed that almost two-thirds (62%) of its suppliers do not comply with its limit of 60 hours per week in the factory. Also, more than a third (35%) of Apple's suppliers do not meet its standards for workplace safety, while nearly a third

(32%) do not comply with Apple's hazmat management practices. To stem the rising tide of criticism, Apple CEO Tim Cook announced earlier this year [2012] that it had joined the Fair Labor Association (FLA) as an associate member, the first high-tech company to do so, and that the FLA will independently report on Apple's supply chain activities.

Speaking at a recent technology conference, Cook said, "We don't let anyone cut corners on safety. If there's a production process that can be made safer, we seek out the foremost authorities in the world, then cut in a new standard and apply it to the entire supply chain."

Ben & Jerry's Scoop:
Fully Fairtrade by 2013

While Apple's secrecy is legendary, at the opposite extreme in terms of outspokenness is ice cream maker Ben & Jerry's, a wholly-owned subsidiary of consumer packaged goods giant Unilever Group. The company has been championing environmental causes dating back to before terms like "green" and "sustainability" ever appeared in corporate reports. One of the company's major commitments is to go fully Fairtrade across its entire global flavor portfolio by 2013, which means all of the ingredients in its ice cream products will be certified by FLO-CERT, which audits companies to ensure that farmers in Third World countries (primarily in Africa) are not being exploited, and that environmentally sound practices are being used to harvest crops in a sustainable manner. Many of Ben & Jerry's products already bear the Fairtrade seal on its packages. On top of the FLO-CERT auditing, Ben & Jerry's also uses a third-party independent auditor that audits the audit.

"This isn't a feel-good operation," explains Jostein Solheim, CEO of Ben & Jerry's. "Our biggest challenge is, there are something like 114 different cocoa varieties. So for each of those, we have to ensure tight quality specifications and the chain of custodianship and our obligations in terms of paying a fair price for the cocoa and that we pay a social premium that will be reinvested in the community of the smallholder farmers. That whole process is why we need partners like Fairtrade International and FLO-CERT to support us."

Quality is always a paramount concern to Ben & Jerry's, and nothing that doesn't meet the company's quality standards will ever go into production, Solheim states. "That's why we build backward in our supply chain, and that's where the overlap in audits comes into play. In terms of supply chain security, there are a lot of benefits in engaging many smallhold farmers because we have a much broader base of suppliers to work with. But clearly, where we can add the most value to the farmers is to move them up the value chain so that they produce a higher quality product and deliver it in a better state to their suppliers, where it then goes into our supply chain."

Unilever Shifts Its Supply Chain to Emerging Markets

In November 2010, Unilever announced its Sustainable Living Plan targets, which included the goal of purchasing 100% of its palm oil from certified sustainable sources by 2015. However, in April 2012, the company announced it had already met that goal, through its purchase of GreenPalm certificates, a trading program endorsed by the Roundtable on Sustainable Palm Oil. Palm oil is a basic ingredient found in roughly half of all products sold in a typical supermarket, from margarine, cereal and cookies to soap, detergent and cosmetics. Palm oil is grown in tropical rain forests, largely in Southeast Asia, and like the FLO-CERT program, the GreenPalm program audits the plantations where the palm oil is grown.

Having reached its initial target, Unilever has now set a new goal: it plans to purchase all its palm oil from certified traceable sources by 2020.

Foxconn

Most of Apple's high-tech products are designed in California, but built overseas, primarily in China, Singapore, and Taiwan, and numerous cases of worker abuse and poor conditions in these facilities have been publicized in recent years. Apple's "Supplier Responsibility" report and annual audit represent the company's effort to ensure that its suppliers adhere to Apple's Supplier Code of Conduct. Foxconn was one of the Apple suppliers audited in 2010. After the scandal over the suicides at Foxconn erupted in 2010, Apple executives traveled to Shenzhen to examine the facilities and interview more than one thousand employees. Although Foxconn was not found to be in violation of Apple's supplier rules, Apple did terminate business relations with other companies when rules violations were found to be flagrant and auditors determined there was little chance of improvement....

In July 2011, China Labour Watch, a New York-based advocacy group for Chinese workers' rights, released a report on its nine-month investigation into conditions in Chinese electronic factories for such manufacturers as Dell, Apple, HP, Nokia, and Motorola. The report charges that not only were workers treated unethically and exploitatively, but also that the conditions in the plants were violations of Chinese law. In January 2012, an estimated three hundred Foxconn employees at a plant in Wuhan threatened to commit suicide in protest against poor wages and working conditions. Foxconn officials announced on 12 January that they had settled the dispute with their workers, stating, "The welfare of our employees is our top priority."

"Sweatshops," Global Issues in Context Online Collection, *2013.*

"What this means is, we'll be able to track the palm oil that we use in a factory, let's say, in Brazil, back to the plantation on which it was originally grown," explains Gavin Neath, Unilever's senior vice president of sustainability. He adds, though, that achieving this new goal will be both difficult and complicated.

"First, we buy a lot of palm oil, roughly 1.5 million tons," he says. "Also, the bulk of our usage is not in so-called 'straight palm' [i.e., vegetable oil], which might be the case for a cookie manufacturer, but as a feedstock to make certain kinds of oleo-based chemicals, which are used in our shampoos, body lotions and other personal care products."

To improve its visibility into the palm oil supply chain, Unilever plans to purchase a fractionation plant in Indonesia for roughly $130 million, which will be involved in the initial separation process of the raw palm oil. Most of the palm oil Unilever purchases comes from Indonesia. "This will give us a much better line of sight into where this material has come from," Neath says. From the fractionation plant, the palm oil will then be sent on to other chemical companies, which will do the further refining that's necessary.

In evaluating where to locate its plants, whether they're making intermediate ingredients or finished products, Unilever evaluates a whole series of factors, Neath points out. "One is proximity to market—where is the biggest market for these products? Manufacturing is being moved from Europe and the United States toward the emerging markets because that's where the greatest population growth is. Another variable is raw materials—where are they coming from? What are the costs of getting them to the factory? Are we dealing with perishable materials? And there are financial considerations as well. Are the governments concerned giving us any incentives to set up manufacturing in that locality?"

Paul Polman, Unilever's CEO, says, "Sustainable growth will be the only acceptable model of growth in the future." To that end, one of Unilever's stretch goals is to cut by 50% the amount of water associated with the consumer use of its products by 2020. "Our plan presupposes that society and government will move with us," Neath says. "We are stone-cold certain that in the next 10 to 20 years, people will be paying much more for water and for carbon. So integrating this kind of thinking now into our business will serve us well in the long term."

Building Credibility Through Best Practices

Air Products and Chemicals Inc., a $10.1 billion supplier of atmospheric, process and specialty gases, addresses what it calls the four pillars of sustainability in its CSR report: environmental stewardship, governance, social responsibility and customer value. As John McGlade, the company's chairman, president and CEO, points out in the report, Air Products spends two-thirds of its annual R&D budget on environmental and energy-efficiency offerings. The company's environmental targets include reducing greenhouse-gas emissions by 7% by 2015 and a commensurate 7% reduction in energy consumption by 2015; a 10% reduction in water consumption by 2015; and a 20% reduction in hazardous waste shipments.

"Ninety percent of what you see in our CSR report is above and beyond what is required of us," points out Corning Painter, who as senior vice president, corporate strategy, technology and supply chain, has leadership responsibility for Air Products' sustainability organization. "There's no legislative requirement on greenhouse gas emissions, for instance.

"Water is a local issue. And while there are rules on how to handle and manage hazardous waste, it was our decision to reduce it by 20%. Like much of industry, we've done things ahead of legislation, and it's in part a feeling that these regulations are coming, so we want to be ready for what comes down the road."

In terms of best practices, Painter points to life cycle assessment (LCA), which takes a systemized approach to calculate the total environmental sustainable cost to manufacture a product, and then offers alternative production processes. In particular, he recommends ISO 14040 as an already-existing framework for LCA, rather than having manufacturers continually reinventing the wheel on things like carbon reduction.

"The more all of industry consistently follows these types of best practices, the more credibility we're all going to have," he says. "Because if 90% of us do it well but 10% don't, and some environmental group finds them out, it will make everybody skeptical of anything that any of us say.

"I think, though, that industry has a story to tell here, and it's a good story. We just need to be out in front of it and let people know that we've all been doing CSR type of activities for a long time."

> *"Given the unprecedented level of glo-
> balisation and the ascent of corporate
> economic might, the development of in-
> ternational norms and enforcement
> mechanisms for the accountability of
> non-state actors is essential to advanc-
> ing justice and long overdue."*

Kiobel Case:
Corporate Accountability for
Human Rights Abuses

Lauren Carasik

*Lauren Carasik is director of the International Human Rights
Clinic at Western New England University School of Law. In the
following viewpoint, she reflects on the importance of the case of
Kiobel v. Royal Dutch Petroleum, the first time the issue of corporate liability in human rights abuses on foreign soil reached
the US Supreme Court. In the* Kiobel *case, Carasik explains,
nine environmental activists protesting oil exploration in the Niger Delta were tortured and murdered by the corrupt Nigerian
government, allegedly with the complicity of Royal Dutch Petroleum. Carasik finds that the* Kiobel *case exemplifies the lack of*

consistent, effective, and accessible solutions to the human rights abuses associated with the activities of transnational corporations. She argues that the best solution is to hold these corporations accountable for such egregious behavior by enforceable legal measures. Corporations that practice corporate social responsibility (CSR) and protect human rights all over the world deserve a competitive advantage and the recognition of the international community for doing the right thing, according to Carasik.

As you read, consider the following questions:

1. When was the Alien Tort Statute (ATS) enacted?

2. How many of the world's 100 largest economic entities are corporations?

3. According to Carasik, what are the goals of the Extractive Industries Transparency Initiative (EITI)?

The United States Supreme Court is poised to issue a ruling in the case of *Kiobel v Royal Dutch Petroleum*. The stakes are enormous—the case will determine whether victims of human rights abuses on foreign soil, who often lack any other viable legal remedy, can bring suit against corporations in US courts.

The underlying facts of the *Kiobel* case are deeply disturbing. In the 1990s, the Movement for the Survival of the Ogoni People was comprised of a group of activists advocating for environmental and social justice surrounding oil exploration by Royal Dutch Shell and its subsidiaries in the Ogoni region of the Niger Delta. Amid severe repression, nine members of the movement, including Dr Barinem Kiobel, were arrested, charged with specious crimes, tortured and summarily hanged. Dr Kiobel's widow Esther and 11 other plaintiffs, all either victims of torture or relatives of victims residing in the US brought a class action suit in the US District Court.

According to the plaintiffs, Royal Dutch Petroleum, parent company of Shell, was complicit with the brutal Nigerian dictatorship in "a widespread and systematic campaign of torture, extrajudicial executions, prolonged arbitrary detention, and indiscriminate killings constituting crimes against humanity to violently suppress this movement".

The suit was brought under the Alien Tort Statute (ATS), a law enacted in 1789 to confer jurisdiction on the federal courts to hear claims brought by non-US citizens alleging violations of international law. The ATS was an obscure statute that had been dormant for almost two centuries until a pioneering lawsuit filed by the family of Joelito Filartiga—the 17-year-old son of a Paraguayan activist who was tortured and killed by a police inspector, who was by then a resident in the US.

In 1980, the Second Circuit Court of Appeals held in *Filartiga v Pena Irala* that the ATS conferred jurisdiction for violations of universally accepted human rights norms committed by actors vested with official authority.

Several decades passed before the next ground-breaking development in ATS litigation, when victims of the Burmese military junta sued Unocal for its complicity with widespread and egregious abuses committed during construction of a transnational oil pipeline, including murders, rape, violent evictions and forced labour. After years of legal posturing, the case ultimately settled in 2004 for an undisclosed sum, and plaintiffs were compensated for the abuses they suffered. The case's success prompted dozens of other victims of human rights abroad to seek justice from corporations under the ATS.

Human Rights Violations

The *Kiobel* case is the first time the issue of corporate liability under the ATS has reached the Supreme Court. In 2010, the Second Circuit Court of Appeals, the same court that created the *Filartiga* precedent, held in *Kiobel* that the ATS did not apply to corporations. On appeal, the Supreme Court initially heard arguments on the threshold jurisdictional issue of the statute's applicability to corporations, and then requested supplemental briefs on whether the ATS allowed for the extra-territorial application of US laws, which many observers considered to be settled law.

The Court held in *Sosa v Alvarz Machain* that the ATS applies to foreign violations of international [law] that are recognised as "specific, universal and obligatory", and courts have applied the ATS to violations such as such as genocide, crimes against humanity, torture and summary execution. *Kiobel* plaintiffs argued that the violations they suffered are universally recognised and condemned harms under customary international law. In its defence, Shell argued that "the law of nations" does not recognise corporate liability for human rights abuses and that the ATS does not apply extraterritorially. Legal observers expect a decision in the *Kiobel* case at any time.

In justifying its position against the extraterritorial application of US laws, Shell underscored the "adverse consequences to US trade and foreign policy of a liberal expansion of private causes of action against corporations under international law". It also posited that the costs associated with potential liability "may lead corporations to reduce their operations in the less-developed countries from which these suits tend to arise, to the detriment of citizens of those countries who benefit from foreign investment".

The assertion that all citizens of developing countries in which corporations act benefit from their activities is the subject of withering critique, and not only from the expected critics from the left. Former Republican US Senator Richard Lugar acknowledged the "resource curse" on the floor of the Senate in the debate on the Cardin-Lugar Amendment of the Dodd-Frank Act, arguing:

> "Oil, gas reserves, and minerals frequently can be a bane, not a blessing, for poor countries, leading to corruption, wasteful spending, military adventurism, and instability. Too often, oil money intended for a nation's poor ends up lining

the pockets of the rich or is squandered on showcase projects instead of productive investments."

The US State Department has also supported the law, noting that it advances rather than undermines US foreign policy interests.

Many human rights abuses are associated with the extractive industries, but also occur in the areas of forced labour, environmental degradation, the involuntary displacement of indigenous peoples from their ancestral lands and others violations. In many of these cases, domestic remedies are wholly unattainable for those harmed, for a variety of reasons. The US is not alone in grappling with the liability of transnational corporations for human rights abuses: in path-breaking litigation, Hudbay Minerals stands accused in Canadian courts of complicity in human rights abuses in Guatemala.

The countries, industries and harms vary widely in terms of scope and severity, but they share a disturbingly common theme: the lack of consistent, effective and accessible remedies for the human rights harms associated with the activities of transnational corporations.

Complicating efforts to hold transnational corporations accountable is the fact that companies often construct a series of subsidiary companies that mask their true ownership, make it hard to impose corporate liability. Imposing corporate accountability is further impeded by other factors.

Logistically, many countries in the Global South where many transnational corporations operate lack the institutional and judicial capacity to manage complex litigation. Moreover, subsidiary companies often funnel profits to the parent corporations, leaving them with inadequate cash reserves to satisfy legal liabilities. Lastly, as noted above, governments may be reluctant to send a message of corporate accountability because those in power are often the most direct beneficiaries of corporate activity.

The Concept of Human Rights

The inclination to protect the rights of fellow human beings is as old as civilization, but it was not until the mid-twentieth century that world leaders arrived at the modern-day concept of human rights—those internationally recognized rights that are due to every person, regardless of nation, culture, race, gender, age, or social position, that stand above cultural differences and must be respected and protected by all governments and all people. This international concept of human rights arose in the aftermath of World War II (1939–45), when the horrors of the Holocaust, and its systematic extermination of six million Jews, as well as Romas, homosexuals, and the disabled, prompted world leaders to establish an international organization to promote peace and security. The United Nations (UN) was founded in 1945 amid a call for absolute international standards that could protect people everywhere from crimes against humanity.

In its founding charter, the United Nations adopted the promotion of human rights and fundamental freedoms as one of its principle purposes, but the rights were not specified. In 1947, the UN Commission on Human Rights was formed to draft an international human rights treaty that was more specific. The result was the Universal Declaration of Human Rights, adopted in 1948. The document begins with the statement that "recognition of the inherent dignity and of the equal and inalienable rights of all members of the human family is the foundation of freedom, justice and peace in the world."

"Human Rights," Global Issues in Context Online Collection, *2013.*

Establishing Standards of Liability

International human rights norms have evolved over the past 50 years, though the primary focus has been on the conduct of state actors. Establishing standards of liability for non-state actors must follow suit. The rise of corporate economic power is highlighted by staggering statistics: 51 out of the world's 100 largest economic entities are corporations and the remaining 49 are countries.

In the US, the wealth owned by the Walton family, of Walmart fame, is equivalent to the worth of the bottom 40 percent of Americans. If Walmart's revenue was listed as GDP, it would rank 25th in the world, ahead of the economies of 157 countries. Given the unprecedented level of globalisation and the ascent of corporate economic might, the development of international norms and enforcement mechanisms for the accountability of non-state actors is essential to advancing justice and long overdue.

Various multi-stakeholder initiatives indicate a global concern about the potentially destructive impact of corporate activities on human rights. The UN-backed Guiding Principles on Business and Human Rights represents an acknowledgement by some corporations that they should adhere to the "protect, respect and remedy" framework for safeguarding human rights in their operations.

Concern over the abuses often associated with the extractive industries in the Global South motivated the creation of the Extractive Industries Transparency Initiative (EITI), now implemented by 37 countries. EITI's strategic goals include minimising risk for investors and "strengthening accountability and good governance, as well as promoting greater economic and political stability. This, in turn, can contribute to the prevention of conflict based around the oil, mining and gas sectors". But absent effective access to judicial remedies, these standards are purely aspirational and therefore, unenforceable.

In the US, it seems disingenuous for corporations to argue that they are not natural persons for the purposes of liability under the ATS, while invoking the protections attaching to corporate personhood to justify their desired outcome in the *Citizens United* case. *Citizens United* generated a storm of controversy for holding that the government could not regulate the political speech of corporations by limiting their contributions to political campaigns. Juxtaposing these positions reveals that corporations are attempting to have it both ways: they want to enjoy rights of corporate personhood while avoiding its attendant responsibilities.

In effect, transnational corporations want to be immunised from liability for their conduct beyond the borders of the US, irrespective of whether a remedy is available elsewhere.

The corporations that voluntarily adhere to principles of Corporate Social Responsibility are likely not the vociferous opponents of accountability, and are arguably at a competitive disadvantage when others are permitted to violate human rights with impunity. Given corporate complicity in egregious abuses around the world, respect for human rights should not be a function of voluntary compliance but instead a matter of enforceable legal rights. The international community must demand accountability, and reinforce and reaffirm the practices of corporations that do take seriously the impact of their behaviour.

The Supreme Court's decision in the *Kiobel* case should advance global justice by categorically rejecting impunity for human rights abuses in which transnational corporations are complicit.

Editor's note: In April 2013, the US Supreme Court upheld the lower court's decision that the Alien Tort Statute presumptively does not apply extraterritorially.

> *"Prosperous enterprises stimulate economic growth in the communities where they do business."*

Corporate Social Responsibility Strategies Should Fight Poverty

Mal Warwick

Mal Warwick is a business consultant and prolific author. In the following viewpoint, he posits that corporations offer distinct advantages in addressing the problem of global poverty: Profitable businesses attract substantial capital; profitable businesses hire people; and successful businesses are capable of optimizing resources and maximizing profits. As a result, he says, if a company succeeds, it can greatly stimulate economic growth in its community and provide new economic opportunities for the unemployed and low-income workers. It can also improve access to a range of products and services, including better sanitation, clean water, affordable food, electricity, health care, education, and housing, according to Warwick.

As you read, consider the following questions:

1. According to estimates from the World Bank cited by Warwick, what will be the world gross domestic product (GDP) for 2013?

2. How much of the world's economic activity takes place in the Global North, according to 2012 estimates cited in the viewpoint?

3. According to the *Financial Times*, as cited by Warwick, how much is invested in emerging economies every year?

There's nothing mysterious here. Poor people tell us they're poor because they don't have enough money—and who knows more about making money than business people?

Capital, Jobs, Scale

Private business possesses three overarching and undeniable advantages in addressing the challenge of poverty:

- Profitable businesses attract substantial capital.

- Successful businesses hire lots of people.

- Successful businesses are capable of reaching scale.

These factors are the foundational truths of *The Business Solution to Poverty*, the new book I coauthored with Paul Polak.

However, there are additional factors we believe bolster the economic power of business.

More Expertise, Less Pressure

Businesses, especially well-established companies, often can marshal all the necessary specialized expertise in design, financial management, marketing and other fields that are usually lacking or inadequate in either the public sector or the citizen sector.

Private businesses tend to be less susceptible to political pressure than governments, multilateral institutions and most citizen-sector organizations—especially in countries with weak governments.

Prosperous enterprises stimulate economic growth in the communities where they do business.

Doing the Math

Let's take a look at a few numbers to get a sense of perspective on the issue of development.

Seventy trillion dollars. That's $70,000,000,000,000, or $70 x 10^{12}. This number is the estimated world gross domestic product (GDP) for 2012—clearly a very large number by anyone's standards. And the World Bank's estimate for 2013 is $75 trillion at this writing [October 2, 2013].

Most of the economic activity represented by those numbers takes place in the Global North—about $41 trillion, in fact, or nearly two-thirds of the 2012 total, as compared with the $12 trillion generated by the emerging economies of the South. And every year, according to the *Financial Times*, approximately $1 trillion more is invested in emerging economies.

Investors Find Opportunity in Global South

So, what can we conclude from all this number-mongering? There's already a lot of money invested in the countries we consider poor. Seeking capital for the ventures we propose isn't like asking for money to set up businesses on Mars. Because another $1 trillion is invested every year in the Global South, rich-country investors are obviously eager to find opportunities for lucrative new investments there. Just ask your broker or financial advisor.

Poor people themselves almost always put first priority on making more money because cash is fungible: it can be used

What Is Poverty?

Poverty is the state of lacking such essentials as money, food, water, clothing, and shelter. The American economist Mollie Orshansky defined poverty as being deprived of "those goods and services and pleasures which others around us take for granted." Poverty is a global problem, but there is much debate regarding how to define poverty and how to remedy it in its various forms. Poverty affects both isolated individuals and larger groups of people. It is especially common in developing countries that have yet to establish governmental social programs, civil services, and human rights standards. However, poverty also exists in developed countries.

Poverty is an ancient problem; the plight of the poor and the duty of others to help care for them are discussed at length in the holy books of most world religions. The poor have traditionally been categorized as either deserving or undeserving. The deserving poor were those who warranted sympathy and aid, including orphans, widows, the disabled, and the elderly and infirm. These are people who might now be classed as the structural poor—those who lack political power and resources and are dependent on others for survival. The undeserving were those able-bodied people without employment. Such individuals are often stereotyped by society as lazy or irresponsible, and these attitudes result in social programs designed to aid the structural poor. The distinctions between the two categories tend to blur during economically difficult periods, when many able-bodied people may find themselves unemployed.

"Poverty," Global Issues in Context
Online Collection, *2013.*

to feed hungry members of the family, to invest in planting a more lucrative crop, to educate children, to gain access to legitimate health care, to replace a leaky thatched roof with corrugated tin—or to meet any other pressing need.

And, in the absence of a working social safety net, increased cash comes only from wages or salaries, or greater agricultural productivity enabled by technology, as well as money saved by access to better sanitation and health care.

Ending Poverty

Ending rural poverty is never a simple or easy thing to do, and not every poor family can attain the middle class in today's harsh reality. Subsistence farming is the rule; joblessness is rife. More to the point, factors such as loss of hope, caste or class barriers, alcoholism, drug addiction, adherence to self-defeating religious beliefs, the subjugation of women, the lasting effects of childhood malnutrition and severe physical or mental limitations—not to mention usurious moneylenders and landlords or corrupt and oppressive governments—may make it all but impossible for a family to thrive in any one of the developing countries in particular.

However, by creating new markets that enhance opportunities for livelihood and open access for poor people to products and services such as clean water, nutritious food, electricity, improved shelter, accessible health care and education at prices they consider affordable—and by providing them with jobs in the enterprises that furnish these goods and services— the poverty that holds back such a large segment of the world's population can become a thing of the past.

While improved education, health, political power, infrastructure and nutrition all play important roles, we have no doubt that improved livelihood provides the most direct path to the end of poverty.

It's undeniable, then, that the private sector possesses all the financial and human resources needed to begin ending the scourge of poverty on Earth.

Periodical and Internet Sources Bibliography

The following articles have been selected to supplement the diverse views presented in this chapter.

Emily Chasen	"Taking Corporate Sustainability Reporting to the Next Level," *Wall Street Journal*, November 1, 2013.
Steven Cohen	"The Push Behind Corporate Sustainability Management," *The Huffington Post*, March 25, 2013.
The Economist	"Disaster at Rana Plaza," May 2, 2013.
Pamela Hawley	"Poverty Is Changing, So Should Corporate Social Responsibility," *Fast Company*, April 6, 2012.
Claire Methven O'Brien	"Corporate Respect for Human Rights: Sustainability's New Black?," *The Guardian Sustainable Business Blog*, May 14, 2013.
Auden Schendler and Michael Toffel	"Corporate Sustainability Is Not Sustainable," *Grist.org*, June 2, 2013.
Christopher F. Schuetze	"'There Is No Sustainable Business,'" *New York Times*, February 25, 2013.
Michael Townsend	"If Boards Don't See the Real Case for Sustainability, We'll Get Nowhere," *The Guardian Sustainable Business Blog*, August 21, 2013.
Ellen R. Wald	"The Green-Washing of Clean Energy Branding," *Forbes*, April 12, 2013.
Peter Weiss	"Should Corporations Have More Leeway to Kill Than People Do?" *New York Times*, February 24, 2012.

OPPOSING
VIEWPOINTS®
SERIES

CHAPTER 3

What Economic Issues Surround Corporate Social Responsibility?

Chapter Preface

During the 2012 presidential election, changes in political campaign funding had a profound influence on the US electoral process. The biggest change was the growing impact of Super PACs, which allowed corporations to make unlimited donations to outside political groups. According to filings by the Federal Election Commission (FEC), a total of 266 Super PACs spent more than $546 million dollars on political ads during the 2012 election. Much of this spending was focused on negative ads against specific presidential, senate, or congressional candidates—a trend that was bound to have a significant effect on national, state, and even local elections.

The emergence of Super PACS in American politics was facilitated by two controversial 2010 court decisions, *Citizens United* and *Speechnow.org v. FEC*. Before 2010, the campaign finance system allowed for the presence of only political action committees (PACs), heavily-regulated groups that could raise money to support a specific candidate or cause. Under campaign finance law, individuals could contribute up to $2,500 to a PAC, but corporations and unions were not allowed to give any amount.

Citizens United reformed those rules. On January 21, 2010, the Court struck down all caps on individual donations and held that corporations and unions could also make unlimited donations. A few months later, the decision in *Speechnow.org v. FEC* allowed for the creation of Super PACs, which raised unlimited contributions from corporations, unions, associations, and individuals. In a few short years, the number of Super PACs in American politics exploded. As of August 2013, there were 1,310 such groups registered with the FEC.

The creation of Super PACs gave corporations a prime opportunity to influence American politics—and the 2012 presidential election gave them a chance to exercise that growing power. According to a study by Demos and PIRG (Public Interest Research Group), 11 percent of all Super PAC funds spent in the 2012 election came from corporate donations, totaling nearly $72 million. In fact, corporate donations were the second largest source of Super PAC funding in 2012.

"This evidence shows that the first post-*Citizens United* election afforded corporations and large donors the opportunity to use their wealth to amplify their voices far beyond the volume of the average member of the general public—threatening the basic American principle of political equality—and they took full advantage," the report concluded.[1]

For many, the *Citizens United* decision signaled a corporate takeover of American politics. With corporations able to donate unlimited amounts of money to Super PACs, there has been growing concern that corporations will attain a disproportionate influence over public policy and government decisions.

For supporters of *Citizens United*, however, the decision provided corporations much of the same right to political speech as individuals. Because corporations are comprised of individuals and have interests, these supporters argue that corporations should have the same right to advocate for candidates and policies.

The financial impact of corporations on political campaigns and policymaking is but one of the economic issues surrounding corporate social responsibility (CSR). Topics under discussion in this chapter include the impact CSR policies have on corporate economic performance and the relationship between corporations and job creation.

Note

1. United States Public Interest Group, *Reclaiming Our Democracy: Distorted Democracy: Post-Election Spending Analysis*, November 12, 2012. www.uspirg.org.

> *"Whilst profit may be the end goal for any business, responsible businesses have managed to attract more investors, reduced their risks and addressed stakeholder concerns."*

Corporate Social Responsibility Helps Business

Rob Fenn

Rob Fenn is a sustainability consultant and an associate at the British Assessment Bureau. In the following viewpoint, he suggests that businesses—both small and large—can benefit significantly from adopting corporate social responsibility (CSR) policies. The benefits of CSR are manifold, he argues: Such policies attract more investors, motivate workers, save money, foster innovation, and create a loyal and passionate fan base. Fenn argues that the success many great companies, including The Body Shop and Walt Disney, have had with CSR shows that corporations can do well by doing the right thing. The key, according to Fenn, is to not treat CSR as a corporate initiative, but as a fundamental way to do business. He urges companies looking to take the CSR plunge to start small and build momentum.

As you read, consider the following questions:

1. According to a 2011 sustainability study by Massachusetts Insitute of Technology (MIT) referenced by Fenn, what percentage of corporations cite sustainability as a permanent part of their corporate agendas?

2. According to a Net Impact study cited in the viewpoint, what percentage of workers would take a pay cut to work for a company committed to CSR?

3. How many sheets of paper does the average office worker use per day, according to Fenn?

No longer is the term 'Corporate Social Responsibility' a novel idea amongst businesses. A 2011 sustainability study by MIT showed that sustainability, in the US at least, now plays a permanent part in 70% of corporate agendas.

Organisations such as Unilever haven't simply been championing sustainable business as a form of corporate philanthropy. Since implementing their Sustainable Living Plan, they have increased growth and profits. Quite simply, doing good is good for business.

How have Unilever achieved this growth? By being a responsible, sustainable business, they have saved money (energy, packaging etc.), won over consumers, fostered innovation and have managed to inspire and engage their people.

Benefits of Corporate Social Responsibility

The Unilever success story is well publicised, but it can be hard to identify with a business of such size. However, the great news is that even the smallest of organisations benefit when putting Corporate Social Responsibility (CSR) at the heart of their business.

Whilst profit may be the end goal for any business, responsible businesses have managed to attract more investors, reduced their risks and addressed stakeholder concerns. With there barely being a day in the news where a business hasn't made an embarrassing error of judgement, more interest is being show[n] in business[es] demonstrating Corporate Social Responsibility (CSR).

The benefits from adopting CSR can be less obvious than say, helping the environment. For example, a survey from Net Impact found that 53% of workers said that "a job where I can make an impact" was important to their happiness. Interestingly, 35% would take a pay cut to work for a company committed to CSR.

Examples of Corporate Social Responsibility

CSR isn't about giving money to charity, or just asking people not to print emails for the sake of Mother Earth! First and foremost, businesses exist to make profit, and this isn't meant to change as a goal. The reality is that no organisation operates in isolation; there is interaction with employees, customers, suppliers and stakeholders. CSR is about managing these relationships to produce an overall positive impact on society, whilst making money.

So how do you put CSR into action? Below are a few examples of what businesses around the World are doing.

Making 'Green' Fashionable: The Body Shop

The Body Shop forged a reputation as a responsible business long before it became fashionable. They were one of the first companies to publish a full report on their CSR initiatives thanks to founder Anita Roddick's [deceased as of 2007] passionate beliefs of environmental protection, animal rights, community trade and human rights. The company has gone so far as to start The Body Shop Foundation, which supports fellow pioneers who would normally struggle to get funding.

Over 20 years ago the company set up a fair trade programme, well before the term 'Fair Trade' started to become

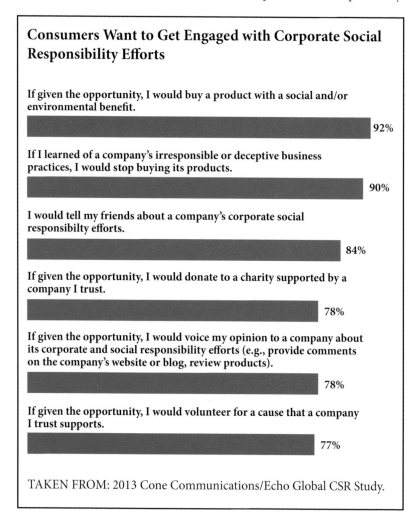

Consumers Want to Get Engaged with Corporate Social Responsibility Efforts

If given the opportunity, I would buy a product with a social and/or environmental benefit.

92%

If I learned of a company's irresponsible or deceptive business practices, I would stop buying its products.

90%

I would tell my friends about a company's corporate social responsibilty efforts.

84%

If given the opportunity, I would donate to a charity supported by a company I trust.

78%

If given the opportunity, I would voice my opinion to a company about its corporate and social responsibility efforts (e.g., provide comments on the company's website or blog, review products).

78%

If given the opportunity, I would volunteer for a cause that a company I trust supports.

77%

TAKEN FROM: 2013 Cone Communications/Echo Global CSR Study.

popular on supermarket shelves. Of course, The Body Shop is famous for its anti-animal testing stance. Whilst this makes testing their products more difficult, especially in markets such as the USA and Japan, their position has created a loyal customer base. The results? From opening her first store in 1976, 30 years later An[ita] Roddick's empire was taken over by L'Oreal for £652m [about $1.08 billion], where it has continued to make annual profits of over £40m [about $66 million.

Putting the Fun into CSR: Walt Disney

Moving beyond making cartoons, today the Walt Disney Company additionally owns the ESPN and ABC networks, holiday resorts and publishing businesses to name a few. The result is a lot of social and environmental impact, as well as the ability to influence a huge amount of people.

Importantly, Disney recognised that you can't entertain a family on the one hand and then disregard the world and circumstances in which they live. Acting responsibly gives the company credibility and authenticity. Accordingly, they have set themselves strict environmental targets and disclose their figures in the Global Reporting Initiative which provides a comprehensive set of indicators covering the economic, environmental and ethical impacts of a company's performance.

Setting ambitious financial targets together with environmental performance targets may sound like an oxymoron, but Disney has managed to do this with initiatives such as running Disneyland trains on biodiesel made with cooking oil from the resort's hotels. They also created the 'Green standard' to engage and motivate employees in reducing their environmental impact when working, having meetings, travelling and eating lunch. With more than 60,000 staff, the results are enormous when everyone is pulling in the same direction.

A clear example of financially benefiting from reducing environmental impact is made with this simpl[e] statistic: a 10% reduction in the corporation's electricity use is enough to power the annual consumption of 3 of their theme parks. Whilst their CSR efforts may have taken a great deal of organisation, dedication and investment, 2012 was a record year for Disney's profits.

Haagen-Dazs and Honeybees

This might sound odd at first, but honeybees are an important part of the global food chain as they pollinate one-third of all the food we eat! With numbers lower than ever, this is bad news for companies such as Haagen-Dazs and their all-natural ice creams. To raise awareness, they created a website, started a social media campaign and donated a portion of proceedings to research.

As you can see, a campaign like [this] works fantastically from a number of different angles. Not only is it helping society as a whole, in keeping with the company's CSR goals, it helps to show a human side to consumers, which can't hurt sales. In fact, research shows consumers are more likely to pay a premium for a product linked to a charity donation.

How can CSR translate to a smaller business? The issues are the same, just on a smaller scale. The key is to start by conducting a review of what impacts your business has. This could be from environmental issues (energy use, waste etc.), to how your employees are treated, your supply chain and the local community. Below is a look at some examples a small business would recognise, and could act on.

The Environment

Even the smallest of office-based businesses can make big changes when it comes to the environment. When you consider an average office worker can use up to 11 sheets of paper a day, are you really reusing and recycling as much as you could?

A common lapse is forgetting to turn off your PC's monitor come home time. Left on overnight, that is the equivalent of printing 800 A4 pages! Multiply that by the varying IT equipment in your office and you're looking at a lot of unnecessary energy use.

The above examples ideally illustrate how thinking sustainability isn't just good for the environment; it saves overheads and helps the bottom-line too.

Staff Welfare

For a smaller business, extravagances can be hard to justify. However, happier staff doesn't simply mean bonuses and pay rises.

What employees value is participation: do they get a fair say? Keeping staff updated on the business and inviting opinions keeps them motivated and loyal. Investing in them with internal and external training helps them do a better job and helps in retraining them, too. Would you rather invest less and have a poor performing, unmotivated team with a high attrition rate instead?

Community

You can incorporate your staff welfare plans with your aims to boost community relationships too. If you'd like to support a local charity, why not let your staff vote for their favourite? It's now common for businesses to allocate charity days where staff get hands-on [time] with their chosen charity, the effects going far further than monetary donation.

In uncertain financial times, employment rates are always an issue. Could your business offer part-time work or training to those in long-term employment, or students looking for their first work experience?

Finally, there's the supply chain. Do you have a policy to purchase locally? With the internet opening up the world, it's surprising how far away some suppliers are. Not only could sourcing locally boost the local economy, you're helping the environment by avoiding unnecessary travel and consequent emissions.

It's surprising when you break down your organisation's activities to see how many people are affected by it. It's also clear that CSR isn't a cynical marketing ploy for big businesses; there are tangible benefits to be had by all. The key is not to treat CSR as an 'initiative', but to simply view it as the way you do business. Applying CSR is just redefining aspects of what you're already doing; it needn't be exotic or costly. Instead, start small and gain momentum.

> *"[CSR] has not always been the boon to profitability for corporations that its promoters promise."*

Corporate Social Responsibility Hurts Business

James M. Roberts

James M. Roberts is the research fellow for economic freedom and growth at the Heritage Foundation. In the following viewpoint, he deems corporate social responsibility (CSR) to be a cynical marketing ploy that funnels much-needed funds away from core business functions and into projects that do little more than polish their brand. Roberts views CSR as part of a disturbing trend toward public-private partnerships, which he perceives as movement toward corporate socialism. Corporations are being bullied into adopting CSR at the expense of maximizing profits, which should be the primary goal, according to Roberts. He says businesses should concentrate on increasing profits and pleasing shareholders, and then publicize the ensuing positive results, such as additional jobs, enhanced benefits for workers, improved environmental impacts, and more investment in the community. Roberts argues that consumers should be better informed about the costs of CSR, and CSR companies should be more transparent about those costs.

As you read, consider the following questions:

1. According to Roberts, what is Wal-Mart imposing on its 100 suppliers?

2. What non-profit organization does Roberts identify as responsible for determining fair traders?

3. What American corporation does Roberts cite as a good role model with regard to applying CSR?

Corporate Social Responsibility (CSR) departments are much in vogue among Fortune 500 companies, but what do they really do? In Africa, Asia, Latin America, and elsewhere around the world, large corporations frequently boast about the social welfare CSR projects they fund as a way for them to "give back." Such comments raise this question: If these corporations are so flush with cash, why don't they reinvest it to grow their businesses, or "give it back" to their customers in the form of lower prices or their shareholders as dividends?

The answers vary. In emerging market countries where government institutions are weak, large corporations use CSR projects to curry favor with local politicians. For many corporate executives in the developed world, CSR is merely a way to polish their brands and inoculate their companies from leftist critics.

In any case, the bottom-line reality is that CSR efforts are just the most visible signs of a growing and disturbing trend toward "public-private partnerships," the goal of which is the transformation of free-market capitalism into a sort of corporate socialism. In essence, these large corporations are at risk of becoming transnational, quasi-governmental entities and (wittingly or not) instruments of state policy implementation. The funds they invest in CSR projects are the functional equivalent of taxes on their customers over which the voters have no say.

CSR: Capitalists Subverting Capitalism

Surprisingly, there is an excellent summary of CSR's broad objectives available on the Web site of that quintessentially American entrepreneurial success story, Wal-Mart, which among other things is imposing a "Sustainability Index" on its 100,000 suppliers. Wal-Mart claims the index will allow it to be supplied "100 percent by renewable energy, creating zero waste, and selling sustainable products."

The very first category in the Sustainability Index is "Energy and Climate," and it requires Wal-Mart's vendors to report their greenhouse gas emissions to something called the "Carbon Disclosure Project." Apparently Wal-Mart executives accept at face value the dire warnings from global warming alarmists about CO_2 emissions—even though there has been little or no global warming since 1997 despite increasing carbon dioxide emissions.

Wal-Mart also ignores Heritage Foundation estimates that the Waxman-Markey "cap and trade" climate bill currently [2009] before Congress would reduce U.S. GDP by $393 billion annually while costing an American family of four nearly $3,000 each year. That is $3,000 in disposable annual income that will not be available to future Wal-Mart customers, but perhaps Wal-Mart executives believe the public relations value of being green will offset this shrinkage of their potential market.

"Fair Trade": The Latest Way to Say, "Look for the Union Label"

In the 1970s, the International Ladies' Garment Workers Union created a memorable jingle urging consumers to "look for the union label." The 21st-century equivalent is the "fair trade" label. Wal-Mart, Starbucks, and many other U.S. retailers now boast that they sell "socially-and-environmentally responsible Fair Trade" products such as bananas and coffee, but who decides which traders are fair? Wal-Mart leaves that up to Trans-

Fair USA, a non-profit organization self-described as "the only independent, third-party certifier of Fair Trade products in the U.S. and one of 20 members of Fairtrade Labelling Organizations International (FLO)."

The organizations behind FLO, however, comprise the usual suspects: far-left, anti-globalization groups and the international trade union movements. Further investigation reveals that "fair trade" is little more than naked protectionism dressed up with humanitarian concern. There is little transparency about how the labor syndicates organized by "fair trade" in commodity-producing countries operate.

Meanwhile, however, Wal-Mart can point to its "fair trade" efforts as a distraction even as it continues to resist pressure from U.S. organized labor to allow unionization of its U.S. stores, a much bigger concern that would raise prices, hurt customers, and threaten Wal-Mart's survival.

Distracted From Their Main Mission

Although efforts to become more energy-efficient, reduce waste, and cut packaging costs should be applauded, former U.S. Labor Secretary and current Heritage Foundation Scholar Elaine Chao points out that the left is using shareholder resolutions to bully corporate executives into adopting some of the more extreme CSR standards—at shareholders' expense.

Indeed, CSR has not always been the boon to profitability for corporations that its promoters promise. David Vogel, a business professor at Berkeley who has studied CSR, reports that Starbucks and other high-profile CSR companies (e.g., Levi Strauss, Gap, Whole Foods, Timberland, and BP—now "Beyond Petroleum" but formerly known more modestly as "British Petroleum") have not done as well financially lately as have other, better-managed firms like Exxon-Mobil that keep their focus on the optimum performance of their core mission instead of seeking CSR-related publicity.

What Is Fair Trade?

In economics, fair trade involves changing trade rules between countries or allowing countries to protect certain interests through trade barriers. In marketing, fair trade refers to a group of practices intended to protect the interests of small producers in the developing world from what are considered unfair prices paid for tropical commodities and goods by companies from the developed world. Fair trade is an attempt to address the price problem that small farmers in the developing world face in that they have no market power so they are price takers. Marketing cooperatives, marketing boards, and a variety of other measures have been utilized in the past in attempts to secure higher prices for small farmers. Some of these practices are based in [the] dependency theory, an economic theory that states tropical countries face declining terms of trade for their bulk commodities. Fair trade employs third-party certification to gain access to fast growing, high value markets. Critics of certified fair trade state that small farmers' rights continue to be violated or that free trade would offer more benefits for small farmers in the developing world.

Blake Stabler, Food: In Context, Gale Group 2011.

Consequently, companies such as Starbucks and Wal-Mart should be more transparent about the costs of their philanthropy by providing more details about prices of their CSR-related products, so that consumers can see exactly how much is being added to the cost of goods to subsidize labor unions and fund price-distorting producer agreements. They can then decide for themselves whether it is worth it. Betsy Atkins of *Forbes* magazine provides a good example to illustrate this point:

It would be very easy to carry out a litmus test of the market for corporate social responsibility. For example, Apple Computer could sell one iPod for $99 and another for $125. The company could announce that the extra $26 from the more expensive iPod would be spent to promote specific social causes, such as education, environmentalism, etc. Such a test would account clearly and honestly for how shareholders' money was being used and would allow the market to drive the outcome. If consumers wanted to pay the extra $26, voting with their wallets for a cause they believe in, they could.

Rather than seeking a public relations coup through CSR, corporations would do better to focus on their primary goals—providing the highest quality goods and services to their customers at the best possible price while earning a good return for their shareholders—and *then* telling the world about the ensuing positive results. A good role model for such an approach is Microsoft, which fought tooth-and-nail for profits and market share. Later, Bill Gates decided to "spread" some of his considerable wealth around through his foundation, but at least it was his fortune, fairly earned, and not unpaid corporate dividends.

The Way Forward

Companies should remain focused on their core mission: increasing profits and providing value to shareholders. As part of this mission, CSR operations should be more transparent. Perhaps corporations should voluntarily adopt disclosure standards similar to those used for nutritional labeling—prices for their products could be broken down to show consumers how much above world price they are paying to subsidize CSR activities. And corporations should insist that "Fair Trade" organizations also publish audited accounts of their operations. Additionally:

- Consumers should be better informed about the true costs and benefits of CSR;

- Shareholders should hold accountable corporate Boards of Directors and demand transparent accounting for CSR activities; and

- Politicians should cease using CSRs to avoid making tough budget decisions, and instead fund essential government services through normal transparent processes of taxation rather than through arm-twisting their corporate cronies.

> *"Is this [perspective on the role of business] just window dressing, a new spin on PR and marketing?"*

Are Companies Responsible for Creating Jobs?

John Bussey

John Bussey is executive business editor of the Wall Street Journal. *In the following viewpoint, he argues that corporations create jobs because it is central to their core mission to increase profits and satisfy shareholders, not because it is part of a corporate social responsibility (CSR) program. Bussey refers to the influential ideas of economist Milton Friedman, who asserted that "there is one and only one social responsibility of business—to use its resources and engage in activities designed to increase its profits so long as it stays within the rules of the game." In recent years, Bussey states, a number of corporate leaders have challenged Friedman's statement, including the CEOs of Starbucks and Whole Foods, but many economists and business leaders still support the basic idea that economic growth creates jobs, not the other way around. CSR may succeed in generating goodwill between corporations and the community, Bussey concludes, but businesses create jobs by paying attention to the bottom line: maximizing profits and reinvesting in the business.*

As you read, consider the following questions:

1. According to a 2011 CNN poll, what percentage of Americans favored the Occupy Wall Street demonstrations?

2. How much money did the Starbucks Foundation donate to a group that helps finance local businesses, according to Bussey?

3. How many Americans does Bussey say were unemployed in 2011?

For anyone stepping gingerly through the encampment of Occupy Wall Street in Manhattan, it might be easy to dismiss the protest as just a living diorama of a 1960s Happening. That is, were it not for its intriguing challenge to American business, and Milton Friedman.

Let's stipulate that the demonstrators have a fuzzy agenda. It's a smorgasbord of gripes ranging from income inequality to poor housing to executive pay—viewed as out of touch with executive value, which maybe we should stipulate too. The protest is diffuse, and young, and cohabitating under tarps. A passerby guiding his three children through the thicket of tents is overheard saying to his wife: "Let's get outta here before the kids see something they shouldn't."

But what about one of the group's chief beefs: that business is falling short of its social responsibility, including creating jobs at home? Some politicians have given a nod of legitimacy to the protests. A CNN poll found that 32% of Americans favor the demonstrations while many others are still making up their minds.

Milton Friedman, the Nobel laureate economist, blasted the very idea of corporate social responsibility four decades ago, calling it a "fundamentally subversive doctrine." Speaking for many capitalists then and now, he said, "there is one and only one social responsibility of business—to use its resources

Milton Friedman's Influence

One of the premiere economists in the late 20th century, Milton Friedman [promoted] economic policies [that] were favored by many country leaders, including President Ronald Reagan of the United States, Prime Minister Margaret Thatcher of the United Kingdom, and military dictator Augusto Pinochet of Chile. His 30-year tenure at the University of Chicago ushered in a new school of economic thought that produced several scholars and economic leaders who went on to win Nobel prizes. Friedman himself would win the Nobel Prize in 1976. Allan H. Meltzer, an economic scholar at Carnegie Mellon University, told the *Los Angeles Times*, "He was a great man. It's hard to think of anybody who never held a government position of any importance who influenced our country—and the whole world—as much as he did."

"Milton Friedman," Newsmakers, *2008.*

and engage in activities designed to increase its profits so long as it stays within the rules of the game."

Companies shouldn't spend profits on unrelated job creation or social causes, he said. That money should go to shareholders—the owners of the companies. Pronouncements about corporate social responsibility, he added, are the indulgence of "pontificating executives" who are "incredibly shortsighted and muddleheaded in matters that are outside their businesses." And that indulgence can lead to inefficient markets.

What then to make of Howard Schultz, the chief executive of Starbucks, who in a letter earlier this month to fellow business leaders asked them to help "get Americans back to work and our economy growing again."

He described Starbucks's own growth and hiring plans—a net of several thousand new jobs—and announced a $5 million donation by the Starbucks Foundation to a group that helps finance local businesses. Starbucks will also encourage customers and employees to donate. He's calling the program "Create Jobs for USA." Occupy Wall Street would like this.

In a blog post last week, Mr. Schultz elbowed aside Mr. Friedman's triumph of profit: "Companies that hold on to the old-school, singular view of limiting their responsibilities to making a profit will not only discover it is a shallow goal but an unsustainable one," the post on the *Harvard Business Review* website read. "Values increasingly drive consumer and employee loyalties. Money and talent will follow those companies whose values are compatible."

Is this just window dressing, a new spin on PR and marketing? A group of CEOs and executives from large companies, including Exxon, Cisco and McDonald's, echo Mr. Schultz's view, though perhaps with a tighter link between largess and corporate self interest.

The group, through their New York-based Committee Encouraging Corporate Philanthropy, highlights projects such as Wal-Mart's effort to reduce packaging in its supply chain (good for the environment, good for Wal-Mart's costs); IBM's "Service Corps," which sends young executives to help developing countries (good for the countries, good for scouting for future IBM business) and PepsiCo's program to train corn farmers in Mexico (good for the farmers, good for PepsiCo, which needed an improved supply of corn).

To do it right, the group says, companies should pick issues that "are integral to the achievement of larger business goals . . . issues that drive growth or reduce costs" and also help society. That's a higher bar than pure charity.

John Mackey, co-chief executive of Whole Foods, goes a bit farther. In a duel with Mr. Friedman in an issue of *Reason* magazine in 2005, he wrote: "From an investor's perspective, the purpose of the business is to maximize profits. But that's not the purpose for other stakeholders—for customers, employees, suppliers and the community. Each of those groups will define the purpose of the business in terms of its own needs and desires, and each perspective is valid and legitimate."

In that exchange, Mr. Friedman acknowledged the value of corporate goodwill in a community—and tending to it—and counseled business to stick to a tight definition of shareholder interest.

Mr. Friedman died the following year, but clearly his ideas on the subject didn't. Economic growth creates jobs, not the other way around, his adherents say. And it helps if government regulates less.

"Jobs are an input, not an output; they're a cost of doing business, not a goal of doing business," says William Frezza, a Boston-based venture capitalist and fellow at the Competitive Enterprise Institute.

"From the perspective of defending capitalism, if you accept the premise of your opponent that business has to give back to society, you've already lost," he says. "To put sack cloth and ashes on—you've delegitimized capitalism, which is the goal of the protesters. Businesses give back to society every day by pleasing their customers and employing their employees. There's nothing business owes other than selling the best product at the best price."

Down at the demonstration, they've broken out the incense and are starting the drum-athon again.

Over at Starbucks, Mr. Schultz is counseling his fellow CEOs that "business leaders have to step up and do our part."

And across America, the 14 million unemployed are waiting for someone to be right.

| "*Businesses have more incentives to eliminate jobs than create them.*"

Corporations Are Not Job Creators

Dave Johnson

Dave Johnson is an entrepreneur and contributor to Campaign for America's Future. *In the following viewpoint, he states that jobs are created when the demand for a product or service is greater than the existing ability to provide them. Therefore, he says, corporations do not create jobs. In fact, he argues, the structure of the US economy provides an incentive for companies to eliminate as many jobs as they can in order to maximize profits. Johnson suggests that it is the government's role to balance the tendency of businesses to cut jobs with the public interest, which is to create well-paying jobs. He claims that the government does this by setting minimum wages, work hours, and creating and enforcing worker safety rules, as well as putting other regulations in place. Johnson concludes that it is essential that corporations not have the ability to influence the government.*

As you read, consider the following questions:

1. According to Johnson, what wrongheaded ideas result when people think that businesses create jobs?

2. What kinds of things do businesses do to cut costs, according to Johnson?

3. What does Johnson say will happen when corporations are able to influence government decisions?

Businesses do not create jobs. In fact, the way our economy is structured the incentive is for businesses to *get rid of* as many jobs as they can.

Demand Creates Jobs

A job is created when demand for goods or services is greater than the existing ability to provide them. When there is a demand, people will see the need and fill it. Either someone will start filling the demand alone, or form a new business to fill it or an existing provider of the good or service will add employees as needed. (Actually a job can be created by a business, a government, a non-profit organization or just a person doing the job, depending on the nature of the good or service that is required.)

So a demand creates a job. A person who sees that houses on a block need their lawns mowed might go door to door and say they will mow the lawn for $10. When houses start saying "Yes, I need my lawn mowed" a job has been created!

Demand also creates businesses. The person who is filling demand by mowing lawns for people might after a while have a regular circuit of houses that want their lawns mowed every week, and will buy a truck and a new mower and hire someone to help. A business is born!

Businesses Want To Kill Jobs, Not Create Them

Many people wrongly think that businesses create jobs. They see that a job is usually at a business, so they think that therefore the business "created" the job. This thinking leads to wrongheaded ideas like the current one that giving tax cuts to businesses will create jobs, because the businesses will have more money. But an efficiently-run business will already have the right number of employees. When a business sees that more people are coming in the door (demand) than there are employees to serve them, they hire people to serve the customers. When a business sees that not enough people are coming in the door and employees are sitting around reading the newspaper, they lay people off. Businesses want customers, not tax cuts.

Businesses have more incentives to eliminate jobs than to create them. Businesses in our economy exist to create *profits*, not *jobs*. This means the incentive is for a business to create as few jobs as possible at the lowest possible cost. They also constantly strive to *reduce* the number of people they employ by bringing in machines, outsourcing or finding other ways to reduce the payroll. This is called "cutting costs" which leads to higher profits. The same incentive also pushes the business to pay as little as possible when they do hire. (It also pushes businesses to cut worker safety protections, cut product quality, cut customer service, "externalize" costs by polluting, etc.)

This obviously works against the interests of the larger society, which wants lots of good jobs with good pay. And businesses, while working to cut jobs and pay less, need *other* businesses to hire lots of people and pay well, because that is what creates the demand that makes all the businesses work.

Government to the Rescue

This is where government comes in. Government is We, the People, working for that larger societal interest. In our current system—when it works—we use government to come up with ways to balance the effects of the profit motive—which pushes for fewer jobs at lower pay—with our larger need for more jobs at higher pay for us, and for the good of all the businesses. We, through our government, create and regulate the "playing field" on which businesses operate. We set minimum wages, limits on working hours, worker safety rules and other rules designed to keep that balance between profit incentive and demand, and that playing field level. (We also provide the infrastructure of roads, schools, courts, etc. [T]hat is what makes our businesses competitive with businesses in other countries. The individual interest in paying less taxes for this has to be balanced with the larger interest that we all pay more for this, but that is another post, titled, "Tax Cuts Are Theft.")

Corrupted

Obviously businesses in our system must be kept from having any ability whatsoever to influence government decision-making in any way, or the system breaks down. When businesses are able to influence government, they will influence government in ways that provide themselves—*and only themselves*—with more profits, meaning lower costs, meaning fewer jobs at worse pay and not protecting workers, the environment or *other businesses*. And, they will fight to keep their ability to influence government, using the resulting wealth gains to increase their power over the government which increases their wealth which increases their power over the government which increases their wealth which increases their power over the government which increases their wealth which increases their power over the government which increases their wealth which increases their power over the government which increases their wealth which increases their power over the government . . .

Unfortunately this is the system as it is today.

Periodical and Internet Sources Bibliography

The following articles have been selected to supplement the diverse views presented in this chapter.

Mijin Cha	"If Corporations Are People, Why Isn't BP in Prison?" *Demos*, January 31, 2013.
James Epstein-Reeves	"Six Reasons Companies Should Embrace CSR," *Forbes*, February 21, 2012.
David French	"Yes, Corporations Are People," *National Review*, August 12, 2011.
Gary Gutting	"Corporations, People and Truth," *New York Times*, October 12, 2011.
Nick Hanauer	"Raise Taxes on Rich to Reward True Job Creators," *Bloomberg*, November 30, 2011.
J. D. Harrison	"Who Actually Creates Jobs: Start-Ups, Small Businesses or Big Corporations?," *Washington Post*, April 24, 2013.
Mark LeVine	"'Corporations Are People, My Friend . . . ,'" *Al Jazeera*, August 12, 2011.
Lynn Parramore	"The Corporate Job Creator Myth," *AlterNet*, April 5, 2012.
Robert B. Reich	"In America, Corporations Are People and Money Is Speech, but Real Human Protestors Are Getting Pepper Sprayed," *Baltimore Sun*, November 24, 2011.
Cynder Sinclair	"Corporate Social Responsibility: Why It Matters and How to Do It," *Pacific Coast Business Times*, March 8, 2013.
Tim Worstall	"Of Course Corporations Are People: We Couldn't Sue Them If They Weren't," *Forbes*, June 19, 2013.

OPPOSING
VIEWPOINTS®
SERIES

CHAPTER 4

Should Corporations Be Responsible for Health Insurance Coverage?

Chapter Preface

On June 27, 2013, a federal appeals court issued its decision in *Hobby Lobby v. Sebelius*, striking down the birth control mandate, a key component of the Affordable Care Act (ACA), the controversial health care law passed in 2010. The birth control mandate requires companies to provide health insurance coverage that includes free birth control to women. The court's decision was celebrated by business owners who believe that such a mandate would violate their religious beliefs. For supporters of the mandate, the ruling allowed employers to deny health insurance coverage to an employee for religious reasons. For legal scholars, the decision illuminated the debate over the rights of corporations; specifically, the question of whether corporations have the right to religious liberty.

The case against the ACA was brought by Hobby Lobby, a family-owned chain of arts-and-craft stores founded and administered by David Green, a devout evangelical Christian. The company, which employs more than thirteen thousand people in forty-one states, closes on Sundays for religious reasons, generously funds Christian charities, provides free spiritual counseling to its employees, and plays inspirational Christian music in its stores. In 2012 Hobby Lobby filed the lawsuit to challenge the mandate to provide emergency contraception, like the morning-after pill, arguing that emergency contraception was equal to abortion. The company did not object to providing coverage for preventative birth control drugs, like the birth control pill, for its employees.

"These abortion-causing drugs go against our faith," maintained David Green in a phone call with reporters. "We simply cannot abandon our religious beliefs to comply with this mandate."[1]

In its decision, the DC Court of Appeals agreed. In his written opinion on the decision, Judge Timothy M. Tymkovich found parallels between the *Hobby Lobby* case and *Citizens United*, a 2010 US Supreme Court ruling in favor of the concept that corporations have free speech rights under the First Amendment of the US Constitution. "We see no reason the Supreme Court would recognize constitutional protection for a corporation's political expression but not its religious expression," he wrote.[2]

The US Justice Department, however, held a different view. Solicitor General Donald B. Verilli Jr. argued that the court's ruling would allow "for-profit companies to deny employees the health coverage to which they are otherwise entitled by federal law, based on the religious objections of the individuals who own a controlling stake in the corporations."[3]

In her dissent of the decision, Chief Judge Mary Beth Briscoe criticized the majority for its judicial activism. Their reasoning was "nothing short of a radical revision of First Amendment law," she wrote.[4]

Caroline Fredrickson, the president of the American Constitution Society, also underscored the radical nature of the court's decision. "The corporation is understood to be a separate legal entity from the people who own it," she argued. "It's always been understood as such. If the Court concludes that Hobby Lobby is merely an extension of its owners and has the same religious liberty rights they do, then there is arguably no limit to a for-profit business owner's power to flout any law he or she finds religiously objectionable."[5]

On November 26, 2013, the US Supreme Court announced that it would hear the Obama administration's appeal of the *Hobby Lobby* decision in early 2014. In addition, the Court will hear another case, *Conestoga Wood Specialties Corp. v. Sebelius*, which also centers on the issue of corporations and the birth control mandate—but with a very different decision. In the 2013 *Conestoga Wood* ruling, the Third Circuit Court of

Appeals held that a privately held, for-profit business cannot challenge the ACA's birth control mandate on religious grounds.

The right of corporations to exercise religious liberty and deny health insurance coverage for birth control is one of the subjects examined in the following chapter, which explores the relationship between corporations and health care coverage. Other viewpoints in the chapter debate whether the government or corporations are obligated to provide health insurance coverage to its employees.

Notes

1. Steve Olafson, "Hobby Lobby Sues U.S. Government over Healthcare Mandate," *Chicago Tribune*, September 13, 2012. http://articles.chicagotribune.com.

2. Adam Liptak, "Court Confronts Religious Rights of Corporations," *New York Times*, November 24, 2013.

3. Adam Liptak, "Court Confronts Religious Rights of Corporations," *New York Times*, November 24, 2013.

4. Mary Beth Briscoe, "Opinion Concurring in Part and Dissenting in Part, Joined by Carlos F. Lucero," *Hobby Lobby Stores, Inc. et al. v. Sebelius et al.*, United States Court of Appeals, 10th Circuit, June 27, 2013.

5. Sahil Kapur, "Liberals Worry As Supreme Court Takes Up Birth Control Mandate," *Talking Points Memo*, November 26, 2013. http://talkingpointsmemo.com.

> *"Employer-sponsored health insurance, and the overly expensive, wasteful private insurance industry upon which it is based, is in its death throes."*

Employers Should Not Be Responsible for Providing Health Insurance

John Geyman

John Geyman is an author, physician, and professor emeritus of family medicine at the University of Washington. In the following viewpoint, he suggests that employer-based health insurance coverage is unsustainable in the United States and has been on the decline over the past thirty years. Geyman argues that in the years after World War II, employer-based health care plans worked because many workers had long-term job security and including health benefits as a part of employee compensation programs worked well for employers. However, he says, times have changed: Workers have multiple jobs and careers and employer loyalty has dropped considerably. He also points out that employer-based health plans do little to control rapidly accelerating health care costs. Paying for health insurance coverage is a

John Geyman, "Employer-Sponsored Health Insurance: Time to Pronounce It Dead," Physicians for a National Health Program, October 5, 2011. www.pnhp.org. Copyright © 2011 by John Geyman. All rights reserved. Reproduced by permission.

burden on US employers, he argues, and hurts American competitiveness in the global marketplace. The solution is a national health care program funded by broadly shared progressive taxes, Geyman concludes.

As you read, consider the following questions:

1. According to Geyman, what percent of employed Americans could claim to have held their job for ten years?

2. What does Geyman cite as the average amount of family premiums for employer-based health insurance in 2011?

3. According to General Motors, how much does it spend on health care expenses each year?

Although many may think today that we have always had employer-sponsored health insurance (ESI) in this country, that is not the case. While some companies offered coverage in the 1930s, the basic concept gained momentum only after the start of World War II. The war effort required a rapid buildup of industrial capacity in the face of a severe labor shortage as many men went off to war. Employers needed a healthy workforce, and needed to compete for workers. Federal wage and price controls made it difficult for them to offer higher pay, so that ESI became an important recruitment tool. Employers were helped by an IRS ruling that made their costs of ESI tax-deductible; these benefits also were not taxable for employees.

We have had about a 75-year experiment with ESI, but its track record is one of continued decline over the last 30 years—fewer people covered, less coverage for more costs, and less value of that coverage. ESI was more an accident of history than a well-planned financing system for health care. Today, rapidly accelerating costs are the Achilles heel for ESI, both for employers and employees, as they are for the entire market-based 'system' itself.

A Different Time

ESI arose at a very different time than today. Beyond the labor shortage, American business was dominant with little concern about foreign competition, and labor unions were strong. Many workers could reasonably expect to hold their jobs for their working life.

Different Challenges

But those days are long gone. Most workers these days have multiple jobs, even careers, over their working years. By 2002, only about one-half of employed men or women could claim to have held their job for ten years. Loyalty between employers and employees has dropped way off in recent years, part-time workers are not eligible for benefits, and union membership hovers around 10 percent of the workforce.

Decreasing Benefits

These markers show a long decline of ESI, as well as the decreasing benefits to enrollees:

- In 1980, more than 70 percent of employees working more than 20 hours a week were covered; that number fell to 56 percent by 2005, with coverage already unraveling as employers shifted from defined-benefits to defined-contributions.

- Over the 13-year period that Kaiser Family Foundation has been tracking premiums for ESI, employee contributions have increased by 168 percent as compared to increased wages of 50 percent and inflation of 38 percent. One-half of employees of companies with fewer than 200 workers now have a deductible of $1,000 or more for single coverage as compared to 16 percent five years ago.

- Premiums for family plan ESI coverage have gone up by 9 percent this year, triple the increase in 2010; family premiums now total $15,073 on average, of which $4,129 is paid by employees (consider that these costs may have little to do with what employees end up paying for their health care, especially those who are older or have one or more chronic diseases!).

- In 2012, average annual employee premiums for health insurance are expected to go up by another 10.6 percent.

- Many of the so-called ESI plans cannot really be called insurance, since they now pass along so much of the costs of care to enrollees even as the extent of coverage withers away. Retiree and disability coverage are being cut by many companies, and their employees are increasingly being herded into lower-cost networks of providers with quality of care in question. As Dr. Don McCanne, Senior Health Policy Fellow for Physicians for a National Health Program, sums up: "The new national standard in health insurance is unaffordable under-insurance".

Beyond the increasing unaffordability of ESI for employees, employers—big and small—have the same problem with no end in sight. General Motors says it spends about $5 billion on health care expenses each year, adding between $1,500 and $2,000 to the sticker price of every car out the door. That burden is many times higher than what neighboring competitors just across the border in Canada pay for health care, rendering GM much less competitive in global markets. Small business[es] (with fewer than 100 employees), accounting for about 40 percent of the private U.S. workforce, cannot keep up with the growing cost of ESI coverage. The small employer market has been one of the most profitable for private insurers, with premiums climbing by 74 percent between 2001 and 2008.

The State of US Health Insurance Coverage

- In 2012, the percentage of people without health insurance decreased to 15.4 percent from 15.7 percent in 2011. The number of uninsured people in 2012 was not statistically different from 2011, at 48.0 million.

- Both the percentage and number of people with health insurance increased in 2012 to 84.6 percent and 263.2 million, up from 84.3 percent and 260.2 million in 2011.

- The percentage of people covered by private health insurance in 2012 was not statistically different from 2011, at 63.9 percent. This is the second consecutive year that the percentage of people covered by private health insurance was not statistically different from the previous year's estimate. The number of people covered by private health insurance increased in 2012 to 198.8 million, up from 197.3 million in 2011.

- The percentage and number of people covered by government health insurance increased to 32.6 percent and 101.5 million in 2012 from 32.2 percent and 99.5 million in 2011.

- The percentage and number of people covered by employment-based health insurance in 2012 were not statistically different from 2011, at 54.9 percent and 170.9 million.

"Highlights: 2012,"
US Census Bureau, *September 17, 2013.*

The Affordable Care Act (ACA)

The so-called health care reform legislation, the Affordable Care Act of 2010, will not fix this problem. Having handed over a combined employer and individual mandate to the private insurance industry, with minimal regulatory clout, the bill (if and when it is implemented) lacks any semblance of cost containment measures. Federal waivers already give employers whatever they want, as illustrated by a recent HHS ruling that allows McDonald's Corp. to keep its very low limits of annual coverage of just $2,000 a year. Whereas President Obama promised that the average American family would save $2,500 a year on health insurance premiums, the Congressional Budget Office later projected that their cost would only increase.

Adding all of this up, we can only conclude that employer-sponsored health insurance, and the overly expensive, wasteful private insurance industry upon which it is based, is in its death throes. As the Vice chairman of Ford Motor Co. said in 2004: "Right now the country is on an unsustainable track and it won't get any better until we begin—business, labor and government in partnership—to make a pact for reform. A lot of people think a single-payer system is better." Some 50 years ago, Walter Reuther, as the national president of United Auto Workers, saw the future this way:

> "When American corporations reached the point where they couldn't make their business more efficient without making it less profitable, when their dependency ratios soared to unimaginable heights, when they got tens of billions behind in their health-care obligations, when the cost of carrying thousands of retirees forced them to stare bankruptcy in the face, they would come around to the idea that the markets work best when the burdens of benefits are broadly shared."

We have to move beyond denial of this problem, and rein in markets that fail the public interest. We can no longer afford ESI or the private insurance industry. Unless we move past political gridlock on this big issue toward a new partnership between labor, business and government, they can bankrupt us all!

There is an answer, of course, in plain sight—not-for-profit, improved Medicare for All, funded by broadly shared progressive taxes that cost patients, families and business less than they are now paying while assuring universal coverage in a less bureaucratic and more accountable system.

> "When health care is universal, doctors are free to recommend and provide the best care for every patient instead of basing their care on what each patient can afford."

Government Should Provide Universal Health Care

Vyckie Garrison

Vyckie Garrison is an editor, publisher, and writer. In the following viewpoint, she traces the evolution of her attitude on government-sponsored, universal health care after she moved from the United States to Canada with her family. She describes her early disgust with Canada's national health care plan. During a couple of her pregnancies, however, she realized she had been laboring under a number of misconceptions about government-sponsored health care and began recognizing the several advantages of universal health care: There never is that consideration of limiting health care because of unaffordable doctor's visits or top-of-the-line treatments; everyone receives the same level of care and access; Canadians don't have to worry about being tied to a job because of health care; and catastrophic accidents or illnesses will not bankrupt families and individuals.

Garrison reports that universal care has not bankrupted the government; in fact, Canada's finances are in much better shape than the United States' finances. All in all, Garrison deems government-sponsored, universal health care a more fair and effective system than the US employer-based system.

As you read, consider the following questions:

1. According to Garrison, what was the abortion rate in Canada in 2008?

2. What does Garrison say is the Canadian policy on maternity leave?

3. What does Garrison cite as Canada's national debt in 2011?

When I moved to Canada in 2008, I was a die-hard conservative Republican. So when I found out that we were going to be covered by Canada's universal health care, I was somewhat disgusted. This meant we couldn't choose our own health coverage, or even opt out if we wanted too. It also meant that abortion was covered by our taxes, something I had always believed was horrible. I believed based on my politics that government mandated health care was a violation of my freedom.

When I got pregnant shortly after moving, I was apprehensive. Would I even be able to have a home birth like I had experienced with my first two babies? Universal health care meant less choice right? So I would be forced to do whatever the medical system dictated regardless of my feelings, because of the government mandate. I even talked some of having my baby across the border in the US, where I could pay out of pocket for whatever birth I wanted. So imagine my surprise when I discovered that midwives were not only covered by the universal health care, they were encouraged! Even for hospital births. In Canada, midwives and doctors were both respected, and often worked together.

A Shock to the System

I went to my first midwife appointment and sat in the waiting room looking at the wall of informational pamphlets. I never went to the doctor growing up, we didn't have health insurance, and my parents preferred a conservative naturopathic doctor anyways. And the doctor I had used for my first 2 births was also a conservative Christian. So I had never seen information on birth control and STDs. One of the pamphlets read "Pregnant Unexpectedly?" so I picked it up, wondering what it would say. The pamphlet talked about adoption, parenthood, or abortion. It went through the basics of what each option would entail and ended by saying that these choices were up to you. I was horrified that they included abortion on the list of options, and the fact that the pamphlet was so balanced instead of "pro-life."

During my appointment that day, the midwife asked her initial round of questions including whether or not I had desired to become pregnant in the first place. Looking back I am not surprised she asked that, I was depressed at the time (even though I did not list that on my medical chart) and very vocal about my views on birth control (it wasn't OK, ever.) No wonder she felt like she should ask if I was happy to be having this baby. But I was angry about the whole thing. In my mind, freedom was being violated, my rights were being decided for me by the evils of universal health care.

A Growing Realization

Fast forward a little past the Canadian births of my third and fourth babies. I had better prenatal care than I had ever had in the States. I came in regularly for appointments to check on my health and my babies' health throughout my pregnancy, and I never had to worry about how much a test cost or how much the blood draw fee was. With my pregnancies in the States, I had limited my checkups to only a handful to keep costs down. When I went in to get the shot I needed because of my negative blood type, it was covered. In fact I got the recommended two doses instead of the more risky one dose because I didn't have to worry about the expense. I had a wide array of options and flexibility when it came to my birth, and care providers that were more concerned with my health and the health of my baby than how much money they might make based on my birth, or what might impact their reputation best. When health care is universal, doctors are free to recommend and provide the best care for every patient instead of basing their care on what each patient can afford.

I found out that religious rights were still respected. The Catholic hospital in the area did not provide abortions, and they were not required to. I had an amazing medically safe birth, and excellent post-natal care with midwives who had to be trained, certified and approved by the medical system.

I started to feel differently about universal government mandated and regulated health care. I realized how many times my family had avoided hospital care because of our lack of coverage. When I mentioned to Canadians that I had been in a car accident as a teen and hadn't gone into the hospital, they were shocked! Here, you always went to the hospital, just in case. And the back issue I had since the accident would have been helped by prescribed chiropractic care which would have been at no cost to me. When I asked for prayers for my little brother who had been burned in a camping accident, they were all puzzled why the story did not include immediately rushing him to the hospital. When they asked me to clarify and I explained that many people in the States are not insured and they try to put off medical care unless absolutely needed, they literally could not comprehend such a thing.

A Fair System

I started to wonder why I had been so opposed to government mandated universal health care. Here in Canada, everyone was covered. If they worked full-time, if they worked part-time, or if they were homeless and lived on the street, they were all entitled to the same level of care if they had a medical need. People actually went in for routine check-ups and caught many of their illnesses early, before they were too advanced to treat. People were free to quit a job they hated, or even start their own business without fear of losing their medical coverage. In fact, the only real complaint I heard about the universal health care from the Canadians themselves, was that sometimes there could be a wait time before a particular medical service could be provided. But even that didn't seem to be that bad to me, in the States most people had to wait for medical care, or even be denied based on their coverage. The only people guaranteed immediate and full service in the USA, were those with the best (and most expensive) health coverage or wads of cash they could blow. In Canada, the wait times were usually short, and applied to everyone regardless of wealth. If you were discontent with the wait time (and had the money to cover it) you could always travel out of the country to someplace where you could demand a particular service for a price. Personally, I never experienced excessive wait times, I was accepted for maternity care within a few days or weeks, I was able to find a family care provider nearby easily and quickly, and when a child needed to be brought in for a health concern I was always able to get an appointment within that week.

The only concern I was left with was the fact that abortion was covered by the universal health care, and I still believed that was wrong. But as I lived there, I began to discover I had been misled in that understanding as well. Abortion wasn't pushed as the only option by virtue of it being covered. It was just one of the options, same as it was in the USA. In fact, the percentage rates of abortion are far lower in Canada than they are in the USA, where abortion is not covered by insurance and is often much harder to get. In 2008 Canada had an abortion rate of 15.2 per 1000 women (in other countries with government health care that number is even lower), and the USA had an abortion rate of 20.8 abortions per 1000 women. And suddenly I could see why that was the case. With universal coverage, a mother pregnant unexpectedly would still have health care for her pregnancy and birth even if she was unemployed, had to quit her job, or lost her job.

If she was informed that she had a special needs baby on the way, she could rest assured knowing in Canada her child's health care needs would be covered. Whether your child needs therapy, medicines, a caregiver, a wheelchair, or repeated surgeries, it would be covered by the health care system. Here, you never heard of parents joining the army just so their child's "pre-existing" health care needs would be covered. In fact, when a special needs person becomes an adult in Canada, they are eligible for a personal care assistant covered by the government. We saw far more developmentally or physically disabled persons out and about in Canada, than I ever see here in the USA. They would be getting their groceries at the store, doing their business at the bank, and even working [a] job, all with their personal care assistant alongside them, encouraging them and helping them when they needed it. When my sister came up to visit, she even commented on how visible special needs people were when the lady smiling and waving while clearing tables at the Taco Bell with her caregiver clearly had Down syndrome.

More Advantages of Government-Based Universal Health Care

I also discovered that the Canadian government looked out for its families in other ways. The country mandates one year of paid maternity leave, meaning a woman having a baby gets an entire year after the birth of her baby to recover and parent her new baby full-time, while still receiving 55% of her salary and their job back at the end of that year. Either parent can use the leave, so some split it, with one parent staying at

The US Health Insurance System

The United States has the highest per-capita expenditure on health care services and the highest proportion of gross domestic product devoted to health care in the world, but it is unique among industrialized nations because it lacks a national health insurance program. Public insurance in the nation exists only for the aged, disabled, and a certain segment of the very poor under Medicare and Medicaid. A large segment of the US population relies on private health insurance, which is either purchased by their employer or by themselves, directly. But many US citizens are not insured. The US Bureau of Labor Statistics (BLS), which tracks medical benefit statistics, estimated that in 2003 about 45 million Americans lacked health insurance and had to pay for costly medical expenses out of pocket. Germany and the Netherlands are two more industrialized nations that do not provide universal health care to their citizens.

"Access to Health Care," Global Issues in Context
Online Collection, *Gale, 2013.*

home for six months and the other staying at home for six months. I could hardly believe my ears when I first heard it. In America, women routinely had to return to work after six weeks' leave, many times unpaid. Many American women lost their jobs when becoming pregnant or having a baby. I knew people who had to go back to work two weeks after giving birth just to hang onto their job and continue making enough money to pay the bills. Also every child in Canada gets a monthly cash tax benefit. The wealthier families can put theirs into a savings account to pay for college someday (which also costs far less money in Canada by the way), the not so wealthy can use theirs to buy that car seat or even groceries. In the province we lived in, we also received a monthly day care supplement check for every child under school age. I made more money being a stay at home mom in Canada than I do in the States working a close-to-a-minimum-wage job. And none of the things I listed here are considered "welfare" they are available to every Canadian regardless of income. For those with lower incomes than we had there are other supports in place as well.

If a woman gets pregnant unexpectedly in America, she has to worry about how she will get her own prenatal care, medical care for her child, whether or not she will be able to keep her job and how she will pay for daycare for her child so she can continue to support her family. In Canada those problems are eliminated or at least reduced. Where do you think a woman is more likely to feel supported in her decision to keep her baby, and therefore reduce abortions?

Since all of these benefits are available to everyone, I never heard Canadians talking about capping their incomes to remain lower income and not lose their government provided health coverage. Older people in Canada don't have to clean out their assets to qualify for some Medicare or Social Security programs, I heard of inheritances being left even amongst the middle classes. Something I had only heard about in wealthy families in the USA.

Financial Costs

And lest you think that the Canada system is draining the government resources, their budget is very close to balanced every year. They've had these programs for decades. Last year Canada's national debt was 586 billion dollars, the USA has 15.5 trillion dollars in national debt. Canada has about one-tenth the population of the US, so even accounting for size, the USA is almost three times more indebted. And lest you think that taxes are astronomical, our median income taxes each year were only slightly higher than they had been in the States, and we still got a large chunk of it back each year at tax time.

In the end, I don't see universal health care as an evil thing anymore. Comparing the two systems, which one better values the life of each person? Which system is truly more family friendly?

> *"If we want affordable and cutting-edge health care, there's only one approach that will work: open competition."*

Government Should Not Be Involved in Providing Health Care

John Stossel

John Stossel is an author, television commentator, and syndicated columnist. In the following viewpoint, he argues that the solution to America's health care problems is not the creation of a big government program, known as the Affordable Care Act (ACA). Stossel lists what he views as the main problems with the ACA: Costs have risen, patients have less choice when it comes to doctors and treatments, and many Americans have lost their health insurance coverage completely. He maintains that these problems are standard when government becomes involved in health care. To confirm this, he points to Canada where, he says, many people can't find a family doctor and must wait hours in the emergency room to receive medical attention. Stossel concludes that the best solution for the United States is to eliminate government participation completely and let individuals purchase their own plans in a market-based, competitive system.

As you read, consider the following questions:

1. How much does Stossel estimate that America spends per person on health care?

2. According to Stossel, how many Americans no longer have the choice to keep their insurance because of the ACA?

3. How many Canadians say that they can't find a family doctor, according to Stossel?

Any day now, the U.S. Supreme Court will rule on whether the Obamacare [known as the Affordable Care Act (ACA)] insurance mandate is constitutional. Seems like a no-brainer to me. How can forcing me to engage in commerce be constitutional?

But there's a deeper question: Why should government be involved in medicine at all?

Right before President Obama took office, the media got hysterical about health care. You heard the claims: America spends more than any country—$6,000 per person—yet we get less. Americans die younger than people in Japan and Western Europe. Millions of Americans lack health insurance and worry about paying for care.

I have the solution! said Obama. Bigger government will give us more choices and make health care cheaper and better. He proceeded to give us that. Bigger government, that is. The cheaper/better/more choices part—not so much.

Costs have risen. More choices? No, we have fewer choices. Many people lost coverage when companies left the market.

Because Obama Care requires insurance companies to cover every child regardless of pre-existing conditions, Well-Point, Humana and Cigna got out of the child-only business. Principal Financial stopped offering health insurance altogether—1 million customers no longer have the choice to keep their insurance.

Government Control of Health Care

This is to be expected when governments control health care. Since state funding makes medical services seem free, demand increases. Governments deal with that by rationing. Advocates of government health care hate the word "rationing" because it forces them to face an ugly truth: Once you accept the idea that taxpayers pay, individual choice dies. Someone else decides what treatment you get, and when.

At least in America, we still have *some* choice. We can pay to get what we want. Under government health care, bureaucrats will decide how long we wait for our knee operation or cataract surgery . . . or if we get lifesaving treatment at all.

When someone else pays for your health care, that someone else also decides when to pull the plug. The reason can be found in Econ 101. Medical care doesn't grow on trees. It must be produced by human and physical capital, and those resources are limited.

Politicians can't repeal supply and demand.

Call them "death panels" or not, a government that needs to cut costs will limit what it spends on health care, especially on people nearing the end of life. Medical "ethicists" have long lamented that too much money is spent in the last several months of life. Given the premise that it's government's job to pay, it's only natural that some bureaucrat will decide that 80-year-olds shouldn't get hip replacements.

The Future of US Health Care

True, surveys show that most Brits and Canadians *like* their free health care. But Dr. David Gratzer notes that most people surveyed aren't sick. Gratzer is a Canadian who also liked Canada's government health care—until he started treating patients.

More than a million Canadians say they can't find a family doctor. Some towns hold lotteries to determine who gets to see one. In Norwood, Ontario, my TV producer watched as

National Health Care Systems

Many industrialized nations have national health insurance systems. Most national health care plans guarantee minimal national health insurance to all citizens, though some provide insurance only to people with low incomes. Many countries that provide national health insurance allow citizens to purchase supplemental private insurance. Countries that have national health insurance plans include Australia, Japan, China, Cuba, Sweden, Russia, the United Kingdom, Germany, the Netherlands, Austria, Sri Lanka, Chile, Thailand, and Canada. Canada's system is acclaimed for its effectiveness in affording health care access to all, and has been successful in keeping the population healthy, though critics say the quality of health care under a national health care program is diminished. Cuba, a developing nation, adopted a national health care system in the mid-1970s with the revised Cuban constitution, which guarantees everyone the right to health care. The country's population enjoys greater health than many nations of similar or higher economic status.

"Access to Health Care,"
Global Issues in Context Online Collection, *2013.*

the town clerk pulled four names out of a big box and then telephoned the lucky winners. "Congratulations! You get to see a doctor this month."

Think the wait in an American emergency room is bad? In Canada, the average wait is 23 hours. Sometimes they can't even get heart attack victims into the ICU.

That's where we're headed unless Obamacare is repealed. But that's not nearly enough. Contrary to what some Republicans say, we didn't have a free medical market before Obama came to power. We had a system that limited competition through occupational licensing, FDA rules and other government intrusions, while stimulating demand through tax-favored employer-based "insurance," Medicare and Medicaid.

If we want affordable and cutting-edge health care, there's only one approach that will work: open competition. That means eliminating both bureaucratic obstacles and corporate privileges. Only free markets can give us innovation at the lowest possible cost.

Of course, that also means consumers should spend their own money on health care, limiting insurance to catastrophic expenses. Americans don't want to hear it. But that's the truth.

> "Americans understand that the essence of religious freedom is that government can't force people to do things that violate their religious beliefs."

There Should Be a Conscience Clause for Employer-Based Health Insurance

Ilya Shapiro

Ilya Shapiro is a senior fellow in constitutional studies at the Cato Institute *and editor-in-chief of the* Cato Supreme Court Review. *In the following viewpoint, he supports broadening the conscience clause, which allows religious organizations to opt out of the contraception mandate of the Affordable Care Act (ACA). The contraception mandate requires that qualifying health insurance plans would have to cover contraceptives and "morning after" pills, which many religious institutions regard as a violation of their religious beliefs. Shapiro maintains that private businesses should also be exempt from the contraception mandate if it violates the religious beliefs of the company's owners. No one is denying women health care, he points out, they just want the ability to decline covering treatment and drugs that do not conform to religious teachings. He suggests that the debate over the contraceptive mandate is a symptom of the much larger issue—the role of government in health care.*

As you read, consider the following questions:

1. According to Shapiro, by 2013, how many cases were brought to challenge the contraceptive mandate?

2. How many people does the arts-and-crafts chain Hobby Lobby employ, according to Shapiro?

3. What does Shapiro say that the Religious Freedom Restoration Act prohibits?

Soon after the enactment of the Patient Protection and Affordable Care Act of 2010 (ACA), or Obamacare, the Department of Health and Human Services (HHS) announced that qualifying health insurance plans under the law would have to cover contraceptives and "morning after" pills. Many religious institutions—most notably the Catholic Church—objected to being forced to fund products and procedures that offend their religious beliefs. This particular mandate may be among the less costly parts of the Affordable Care Act—as we learned from the Sandra Fluke imbroglio [in which Sandra Fluke, a young woman in favor of the ACA's birth-control mandate, was attacked by several conservative politicians and commentators], birth control isn't that expensive—but it certainly struck a nerve and is the subject of much of the "second wave" of Obamacare litigation.

In August 2011, HHS bowed to political pressure and provided exemptions to certain religious organizations, those that only serve people of their own faith and are engaged only in religious activities. That is, the exemption covers churches—presumably only churches that don't provide social services—but not the panoply of religious institutions, such as schools and hospitals, that aren't purely worship institutions. And it certainly doesn't exempt businesses run by religious people, whose objections are identical: being forced by the government to do something against their religion as a condition of continuing in operation.

Legal Challenges

Accordingly, more than 40 cases challenging the contraceptive mandate are now active across the country by various individuals, religious institutions, nonprofit organizations and small businesses. District courts have split on the lawsuits, though many have dismissed them as being premature—because final regulation has not yet been promulgated and the mandate only went into effect this past New Year's Day.

Two of those suits were consolidated late last year for the first appellate argument on the issue: one brought by Wheaton College, a Christian liberal arts college in Illinois, and another brought by Belmont Abbey College, a North Carolina college based around a Benedictine abbey. The legal point here is somewhat technical, but incredibly important for anyone who thinks his freedom of conscience may be violated by the government in the future (a category that includes essentially everyone).

HHS Response

As noted above, the contraception mandate came to include a narrow exemption for religious institutions, one that wasn't available to religiously affiliated colleges. After the strong backlash against even that "narrowed" mandate, HHS issued a "safe harbor statement," saying that the government wouldn't enforce the mandate for a year (until August 2013) against certain nonprofit organizations religiously opposed to covering contraception. In other words, the contraception mandate is still in place but just won't be enforced—but only for a year and individuals are still free to sue to enforce it against their religiously opposed employers.

© Eric Allie/CagleCartoons.com.

HHS also issued an Advance Notice of Proposed Rulemaking (ANPRM) that announced the department's consideration of more permanent methods of accommodating religious institutions. Because of the safe harbor notice and the ANPRM, the district court dismissed the colleges' lawsuits for lack of standing and ripeness, holding that the colleges weren't suffering any injury and it was too early to challenge the proposed rule. The case thus went to the U.S. Court of Appeals for the D.C. Circuit, where the colleges argued at a December 14 hearing that they are in fact suffering a current injury—having to plan for a Hobson's choice—and that the mere possibility of a future accommodation is too remote to terminate their case.

Legal Limbo

The Cato Institute filed an amicus brief [a statement filed by a party to influence a legal case or issue] supporting the colleges in that technical argument, joining the Center for Constitutional Jurisprudence and the American Civil Rights Union. We argued that the trial court misapplied the constitutional test for standing by not focusing on the facts that existed at the outset of the case; subsequent government actions, such as the ANPRM, are irrelevant to the preliminary question of standing. We also argued that the district court's ruling compromises the principle of separation of powers by allowing the executive branch to strip a court of jurisdiction merely by issuing a safe harbor pronouncement and an ANPRM (which doesn't legally bind an agency to act in any way). It was thus entirely speculative whether the agency would alleviate the harms that the colleges are suffering.

Without intervention from the courts, therefore, the colleges would be left in legal limbo while facing immediate and undeniable harms to their religious freedom: On one hand, they can't challenge the constitutionality of a final regulation. On the other, they can't very well rely on a proposed regulatory amendment that may be offered at some unknown point in the future. The trial court rulings in the Wheaton College and Belmont Abbey College cases were thus frightening examples of judicial abdication that permit the expansion of executive power far beyond its constitutional limits.

The Decision

Fortunately, the circuit court agreed. In a brisk three-page opinion released December 18 (four days after argument), the *per curiam* court held as follows: (1) the colleges have standing because that's assessed at the time lawsuits are filed (here, before the ANPRM); (2) the government's representation that the rule would never be enforced in its current form is "binding"; and (3) the government must update the court every 60 days. Accordingly, the lawsuits shouldn't have been dismissed and are instead to be held "in abeyance" pending "the new rule that the government has promised will be issued soon."

Assuming that the government doesn't act in contempt of court, religiously affiliated nonprofits—or service organizations, or whatever the final wording will be—will thus join religious-worship institutions as exempt from the mandate.

But that's not the end of the matter. Employers engaged in for-profit activity, including those who have the exact same objections as Wheaton and Belmont Abbey, will still be forced to choose between continuing their business and maintaining their religious principles. Most notable among these companies is Oklahoma-based Hobby Lobby, Inc., the art-and-crafts chain that employs 21,000 people and has well over $2 billion in annual revenues.

The Hobby Lobby Case

Hobby Lobby lost its motion for a preliminary injunction against the mandate, the Tenth Circuit declined to issue an injunction pending appeal, and, on December 26—coincidentally St. Stephen's Day, honoring Christianity's first martyr—Justice Sotomayor (as circuit justice) declined to provide such an injunction as well. Thus, when the mandate went into effect last week, Hobby Lobby became potentially subject [to] more than $1 million in daily fines.

That's a shame. If we're to respect religious belief, why does the motive of those espousing them matter for whether the government gets to trample them? The owners of Hobby Lobby donate plenty to charity out of the profits they make, possibly having greater impact than many of the nonprofits that are (or will be) exempt. Even if they didn't, however, this country was founded on ideals of religious liberty that went on to be enshrined in the First Amendment, so why would we just ignore them?

Indeed, when one of these lawsuits finally reaches the Supreme Court—which it will unless at least this part of Obamacare is repealed—the plaintiffs should win without even getting to the constitutional claims. That's because the Religious Freedom Restoration Act prohibits the government from placing a "substantial burden" on the exercise of religion unless it has a "compelling interest" and uses the "least restrictive means" to achieve it.

Americans understand that the essence of religious freedom is that government can't force people to do things that violate their religious beliefs. Some may argue that there's a conflict here between religious freedom and women's rights, but that's a "false choice"—as the president himself like to call such things. If the HHS rule is repealed, women will still be perfectly free to obtain contraceptives, abortions and whatever else isn't against the law. They just won't be able to force others to pay for them.

Imposing Government Values

But there's an even bigger issue here. This is just the latest example of the difficulties in turning health care—or increasing parts of our economy more broadly—over to the government. As my colleague Roger Pilon has written, when health care (or anything) is socialized or treated as a public utility, we're forced to fight for every "carve-out" of liberty. Those progressive Catholics who supported Obamacare, or the pro-life Democrats who voted for it, who are now appalled by certain HHS rules should have thought of that before they used the government to make us our brother's keeper.

The more government controls—whether health care, education, or even marriage—the greater the battles over conflicting values. With certain things, such as national defense, basic infrastructure, clean air and water and other "public goods," we largely agree, at least inside reasonable margins. But we have vast disagreements about social programs, economic regulation and so much else that government now dominates at the expense of individual liberty. Those supporting Wheaton and Belmont Abbey Colleges and Hobby Lobby are rightly concerned that people are being forced to do what their religious beliefs prohibit. But that all comes with the collectivized territory.

"[The] cases before the court raise questions about where conscience can possibly end, and the extent to which at least some of this explosion in conscience clause legislation represents a rear-guard action launched to regain ground lost in the culture wars."

Conscience Creep

Dahlia Lithwick

Dahlia Lithwick is a writer who covers legal issues and the courts for Slate. *In the following viewpoint, she contends that conscience clauses, which allow religious institutions an exemption from providing health insurance coverage for contraception, have led to conscience creep: a systematic and relentless effort to broaden conscience claims so that anyone can claim religious exemption from anything that they say is offensive to their religious beliefs. Lithwick notes that the conscience clause has been used by pharmacists, ambulance drivers, cashiers at supermarkets, and guards at prisons. Organizations and individuals have been allowed to refuse to: provide abortion and birth control, teach AIDS patients, facilitate the unionization of a religious university, and allow private adoptions to same-sex couples. She argues that the religious right is abusing the conscience clause to regain ground it lost in the culture wars, and corporations are abusing it to undermine the social welfare state.*

As you read, consider the following questions:

1. According to Lithwick, what is the Church Amendment?

2. In what year did the Supreme Court decide the *NLRB v. Catholic Bishop of Chicago?*

3. According to a study by Professor Elizabeth Sepper cited by Lithwick, what percentage of physicians report having practiced at religiously affiliated institutions with refusal policies?

Just before they shut down the federal government this week [October 2012], opponents of President Obama's health care law attempted to tweak the thing with a one-year delay of Obamacare, a repeal of the medical-device tax, and a "conscience clause" that would have allowed employers to decline to offer their workers birth control coverage if it offended their religious or moral preferences. As Amanda Marcotte noted Tuesday, [in a *Slate* article published on September 30, 2013], this effort reinforces the "view of the employer-employee relationship, in which apparently your boss' beliefs and views are supposed to be in the mix when you're making personal decisions about how you have sex and procreate."

But what's really wrong with conscience clauses? We all have consciences and laws that exist to protect us from being forced to violate our religious and ethical principles should be welcome on the left and right. The problem isn't conscience clause legislation so much as what we might call conscience creep: a slow but systematic effort to use religious conscience claims to sidestep laws that should apply to everyone. Recalibrating who can express a right of conscience (i.e., do corporations have a conscience?) and what the limits of that conscience might be, may well be the next front in the religious liberty wars being waged in courts around the country.

In the current craze to deploy conscience arguments to scuttle unpopular provisions of the Affordable Care Act, birth control is just the tip of the iceberg.

The Origins of the Conscience Clause

The explosion in conscience claims was kicked off by the decision in *Roe v. Wade*, which led to a national wave of legislation protecting those with religious objections from participating in abortions. States and the federal government rushed to promulgate conscience clauses for health care workers seeking to be exempt from providing or assisting in abortions. Passed in 1973, the Church Amendment provided that "receipt of federal funds did not require an individual or institution to perform sterilizations or abortions if it would be contrary to . . . religious beliefs or moral convictions." Since then, most states and the federal government have passed laws allowing health care providers to opt out of procedures that offend their religious convictions.

But it hasn't stopped at health care providers, and the list of objectors now encompasses pharmacists and ambulance drivers, cashiers in supermarkets and business owners who object to same-sex marriage. Last year, for instance, a prison guard withheld an abortion pill from a prisoner who'd been raped on the grounds that it violated her personal religious beliefs. And it hasn't stopped at abortion, birth control, or sterilization, but may include activities like counseling rape victims or teaching AIDS patients about clean needles.

Conscience Creep

Nor has the creep stopped there. In 2012 the Commonwealth of Virginia joined North Dakota in declaring it a privilege of religious freedom to allow private adoption or foster care agencies to refuse to be involved in any child placement that "would violate the agency's written religious or moral convictions or policies." One proponent of the legislation explained that the purpose of the conscience clause was to "chisel into law the principle that people of faith can adhere to their convictions without fear of reprisal from those who would discriminate against their religious beliefs regarding how we should raise our children." The argument that discriminating against, for instance, same-sex or single parents in placing children in adoptive or foster homes, represents religious liberty should at least be subject to careful calibration and discussion. Religious liberty to discriminate against same-sex parents has a cost, both for thousands of children awaiting adoptive homes, and for basic principles of nondiscrimination.

This past summer, Republicans in the House tried to amend the National Defense Authorization Act to "protect inappropriate, defamatory, and discriminatory speech and actions" in the military. The amendment broadened a "conscience clause" that protected the right of troops and chaplains to hold anti-gay views so long as they did not actively discriminate against gay service members.

And it's not just health workers, and parents, and soldiers, and adoption agencies expressing a right of conscience. Some Catholic universities have argued to the National Labor Relations Board that as religious institutions they should be exempt from regulation under the Wagner Act, under which the right to organize is protected. Hearing about the Duquesne University adjunct who died last month, some readers were surprised to learn that "Duquesne had fought unionization, claiming that it should have a religious exemption. Duquesne has claimed that the unionization of adjuncts . . . would somehow interfere with its mission to inculcate Catholic values among its students." The issue, again a complicated one, is whether Catholic schools can ban unions on the basis that unions would afford the NLRB jurisdiction over religious disputes. In 1979 the Supreme Court held in *NLRB v. Catholic Bishop of Chicago* that religious schools and colleges are exempt from NLRB jurisdiction. Adjunct faculty at small Catholic universities around the country have increasingly begun to question the wisdom of this particular expression of religious liberty.

Refighting the Culture Wars

This term the Supreme Court will most likely hear an appeal from a case in which the religious owners of a secular, for-profit corporation will defend a right of conscience in denying their secular, for-profit employees access to birth control guaranteed to them under federal law. The tensions between the religious freedom clauses and the establishment clauses of the First Amendment are vexing, intractable, and baked in. And nobody is suggesting for a moment that religious individuals should not have the right to zealously protect their religious convictions. But at bottom, the cases before the court raise questions about where conscience can possibly end, and the extent to which at least some of this explosion in conscience clause legislation represents a rear-guard action launched to regain ground lost in the culture wars.

In a thoughtful 2012 piece in the *Virginia Law Review*, called "Taking Conscience Seriously," Professor Elizabeth Sepper talks about the stunning asymmetry of modern conscience protections and the ways they privilege the consciences of some over others. She notes that individual doctors seeking to exercise their right to treat patients as they see fit have their own conscience rights subsumed by the conscience rights of the hospitals and universities by whom they are employed. Sepper takes the notion of religious conscience extremely seriously. But she raises important questions about why some consciences are more important to us than others. She contends that endowing health care and other institutions with conscience rights has privileged those institutions' rights to refuse to provide certain treatments over the rights of individual providers to give care they feel obligated by conscience to deliver. In short, she argues, there is a cost to extending conscience rights to big institutions and entities. And the cost may well be the conscience rights of the actual human people who work there.

Sepper cites a study that shows that 43 percent of physicians reported having practiced in religiously affiliated institution[s] with refusal policies, this despite the fact that many of those health care institutions are not actually affiliated with any religion. She concludes that there is no moral or legal argument for accommodating the rights of those institutions that refuse to treat over those that seek to provide treatment. She offers several suggestions for how the law might attempt to accommodate the consciences of all, rather than just the consciences of some, carefully scrutinizing the cohesion, size, and message of the institution to identify the strength of its conscience claims.

These are some of the questions we need to be posing to ourselves as we think about the phenomenon of conscience creep. Can corporations really have consciences? Can your corporate conscience preclude you from merely paying a tax as required under the ACA? Where does the conscience of a business owner run afoul of her employees' consciences? If conscience clauses—as expressed in statutes that allow large entities to impose their religious preferences upon smaller ones—are the vehicle by which we are going to end-run the most fundamental aspects of the social welfare state, lets at least start from the basic principle that all of us have a conscience, and take it from there.

Periodical and Internet Sources Bibliography

The following articles have been selected to supplement the diverse views presented in this chapter.

Mintaka Angell	"Shutting Down the Conscience Clause," *Brown Political Review*, October 2, 2013.
Jonathan Cohn	"More Government in Health Care? Yes. You Got a Problem with That?" *The New Republic*, January 18, 2011.
Ken Connor	"Refuse to Render unto Caesar," *Townhall.com*, September 25, 2013.
Shikha Dalmia	"Republicans Should Convert Obamacare into a Free-Market System," *Reason.com*, October 1, 2013.
Jim Daly	"Birth-Control Mandate: Beyond Our God-Given Rights," *Washington Post*, February 14, 2012.
Edmund F. Haislmaier	"The Complexities of Providing Health Insurance," *The Heritage Foundation*, February 25, 2013.
Paul Krugman	"Health Care Realities," *New York Times*, July 30, 2009.
Parthiv N. Parekh	"Of Government Role and Universal Health Care," *The Huffington Post*, July 12, 2012.
Randy Pate	"Removing Conscience Rights: A Dangerous Prescription in Health Care," *The Foundry*, April 2, 2009.
Uwe E. Reinhardt	"A 'Government Takeover' of Health Care?," *New York Times*, February 26, 2010.

For Further Discussion

Chapter 1

1. Rose Schreiber asserts that corporate social responsibility is an essential strategy for businesses in today's marketplace. Sudeep Chakravarti argues that it is little more than a marketing ploy. After reading both viewpoints, which argument do you find more persuasive and why?

2. Aneel Karmani argues that responsible corporate behavior can only be influenced through the profit motive. Mahesh Chandra argues that follow international standards of corporate social responsibility are a helpful way for companies to meet the needs of their various stakeholders and contribute to society. James M. Roberts and Andrew W. Markley contend that such standards are flawed and undermine the benefits of the free market. Are social responsibility standards necessary? Why or why not? What should be the guiding principles of corporate behavior? Explain your answer.

Chapter 2

1. Environmental sustainability has been a hot topic in corporate social responsibility. After reading the viewpoints written by Dan Gray and Adam Kingsmith, offer your perspective on the role sustainability should have in business. Should it be a top priority for corporations? What factors could hinder the integration of sustainability into business practices?

2. This chapter examines the key components of a successful corporate social responsibility strategy. Read all of the viewpoints in this section. Which do you feel are most important and why?

Chapter 3

1. What is the ultimate value of a corporate social responsibility strategy to business? Read the viewpoints by Rob Fenn and James M. Roberts to inform your answer.

2. In his viewpoint, John Bussey contends that businesses create jobs because it is a natural part of economic growth and maximizing profits. Dave Johnson counters that business has an incentive to streamline production and cut jobs. Which viewpoint makes the more persuasive argument, in your opinion? Explain your answer.

Chapter 4

1. Should employers be responsible for providing health insurance for their employees? Or would the government be a better option? Use the viewpoints by John Geyman, Vyckie Garrison, and John Stossel to inform your answer.

2. In his viewpoint, Ilya Shapiro maintains that employers should be able to exercise a conscience clause, which would allow them to not provide coverage for medical treatments or medications that violate their religious or moral beliefs. Dahlia Lithwick argues that conscience clauses are bad policy. In your opinion, which viewpoint makes the better argument and why?

Organizations to Contact

The editors have compiled the following list of organizations concerned with the issues debated in this book. The descriptions are derived from materials provided by the organizations. All have publications or information available for interested readers. The list was compiled on the date of publication of the present volume; names, addresses, phone and fax numbers, and e-mail and Internet addresses may change. Be aware that many organizations take several weeks or longer to respond to inquiries, so allow as much time as possible.

Alliance for Research on Corporate Sustainability (ARCS)
Darden School of Business, P.O. Box 6550
Charlottesville, VA   22906
(434) 982-2656
website: www.corporate-sustainability.org

ARCS was launched in 2009 to foster collaboration between leading academic institutions in the field of corporate sustainability. To that end, it sponsors a series of conferences and forums to bring together researchers, facilitate network opportunities, and encourage the exchange of ideas. Research is key to the organization's mission; ARCS "helps develop greater understanding of the opportunities and limits of policies and strategies to create sustainable businesses by facilitating rigorous academic research." The ARCS website features access to this research, including papers, commentary, news, and a blog. Members can also access MapEcos, a web tool that offers detailed information on environmental performance and management.

American Sustainable Business Council (ASBC)
1401 New York Avenue NW, Suite 1225
Washington, DC   20005
(202) 595-9302
website: asbcouncil.org

ASBC is an alliance of American businesses working together to inform politicians, business leaders, and policymakers about the benefits of corporate sustainability and to advocate for policies and opportunities to "foster a vibrant, just, and sustainable economy." The ASBC mission states that socially responsible business practices and strong financial performance go hand in hand and should be the model for American businesses in the twenty-first century. ASBC advocacy focuses on persuading policymakers to remove obstacles to sustainable business practices and supporting private/public collaboration toward sustainable development. The ASBC website features access to news articles, op-eds and commentary, poll results, media backgrounders, an events calendar, a blog, and podcasts of recent radio shows.

Business for Social Responsibility (BSR)
5 Union Square West, 6th Floor, New York, NY   10003
(212) 370-7707 • fax: (646) 758-8150
e-mail: connect@bsr.org
website: www.bsr.org

BSR is a global nonprofit organization that was established to work with business to create a more sustainable world. To that end, it promotes collaboration between businesses and their stakeholders and supports efforts to integrate sustainability into strategy and operations. BSR works with more than 250 of the world's top corporations to inform and enhance their sustainability efforts. BSR plays a major role in research in the corporate social responsibility field, working to identify practices and campaigns that would have a positive effect on both the environment and a corporation's bottom line. Information on these efforts can be found on the BSR website, including *BSR Insight*, a magazine that examines the latest in business and sustainability; a BSR blog; a podcast featuring BSR voices and other experts in the field; and a number of in-depth research reports.

Center for Business Ethics (CBE)
Bentley University, Adamian Academic Center 108
175 Forest Street, Waltham, MA   02452

(781) 891-2000 • fax: (781) 891-2988
e-mail: cbeinfo@bentley.edu
website: www.bentley.edu

CBE at Bentley University is a leading research institute in the field of corporate ethics and governance. Established in 1976, CBE conducts research projects and collaborates with private and public partners to develop ethical practices, concepts, and campaigns for corporations, and educates business leaders and stakeholders on the impact of sustainability and ethical practices in the corporate world. CBE established the Ernest A. Kallman Executive Fellows Program, which gathers several highly respected experts in business ethics to provide invaluable insight into emerging trends in corporate social responsibility and corporate governance. These research fellows take part in a series of conferences on business ethics to present new concepts and share best practices. CBE's website provides access to the institute's quarterly newsletter, *Business and Society Review*, as well as recent surveys, research, and a repository of relevant articles written by Kallman fellows.

Center for Corporate Ethics (CCE)
18 Central Street, Suite 2B, Rockport, ME   04856
(207) 236-6658
e-mail: ethics@globalethics.org
website: www.globalethics.org

CCE is a division of the Institute for Global Ethics (IGE), a nonprofit research institute established in 1990 to promote ethical behavior in the global marketplace. IGE's mission is "to explore the common ground of values, elevate awareness of ethics, provide practical tools for making ethical decisions, and encourage moral actions based on those decisions." The CCE focuses on helping American businesses reassess their ethical behavior to avoid ethical lapses and provides information on best practices, emerging trends, and the benefits of human and environmental sustainability. The IGE website provides access to articles written by senior fellows at the Institute, as well as a number of other IGE publications and resources: *Ethical Connections*, an informative newsletter; *Ethicast*, podcasts of interviews of leaders in the field of corporate governance and commentary from IGE fellows; videos on relevant topics; and *Ethics Newsline*, a recap of key stories from all over the world in the area of business ethics and related subjects.

Council of Better Business Bureaus (BBB)
3033 Wilson Blvd., Suite 600, Arlington, VA   22201
(703) 276-0100
website: www.bbb.org

The Council of BBB is the national council that oversees regional organizations, known as Better Business Bureaus, which are tasked with creating an ethical marketplace for American consumers. BBB is dedicated to setting marketplace standards; identifies, investigates, and publicizes businesses that perpetrate consumer scams and profit by unethical behavior in the marketplace; encourages and supports best practices; offers objective and accurate information to the public on businesses and the marketplace; and denounces businesses that violate BBB standards. If an organization has received BBB accreditation it means that it has been vetted and found to meet BBB's standard of performance and service. The BBB website offers information for consumers on accredited businesses and charities, key articles and tips for consumers, lists of the top consumer scams of the year, a blog, and access to the BBB's e-newsletters, including *Scam Alert, Smart Investing*, and *Wise Giving*.

Government Accountability Project (GAP)
1612 K Street NW, Suite 1100, Washington, DC   20006
(202) 457-0034
e-mail: info@whistleblower.org
website: www.whistleblower.org

GAP is a nonprofit organization founded to "promote government and corporate accountability by protecting whistleblowers, advancing occupational free speech, and empowering citizen activists." One aspect of GAP's mission is to advocate for stronger protections for corporate whistleblowers. It also works to educate workers, executives, and legal staff on the rights of employees, especially in the area of free speech. The GAP website offers access to a blog, *The Whistleblogger*, which features posts that examine topics such as corporate and financial accountability, the environment and corporate sustainability efforts, and the treatment of labor and human rights in the workplace. Recent commentary, op-eds, news, and newsletters can also be accessed on the GAP website.

International Society of Business, Economics, and Ethics (ISBEE)
Center for Ethical Business Cultures
Opus College of Busines
University of St. Thomas—Minnesot
1000 LaSalle Avenue, TMH 331, Minneapolis, MN   55403
(651) 962-4120 • fax: (651) 962-4042
website: www.globalethics.net

ISBEE is a global professional association of leaders from business, law, environmental activism, marketing, economics, philosophy, politics, and other fields that study the intersection of business, economics, and ethics. The organization's mission is to "provide a forum for the exchange of experience and ideas; to enhance cooperation in cross-functional and cross-cultural projects; and to discuss the ethical dimension of economic, social, and environmental issues which affect companies nationally and internationally." ISBEE sponsors regional conferences and the ISBEE World Congress, which brings its diverse group of members together for networking purposes and to disseminate the latest research and trends in corporate social responsibility.

US Green Chamber of Commerce (USGCC)
249 S. Highway 101, #420, Solana Beach, CA   92075
(858) 222-2320
e-mail: info@usgreenchamber.com
website: www.usgreenchamber.com

USGCC was established in San Diego in 2009 to support and facilitate sustainable business practices in American business. To this end, it provides a number of networking opportunities, allowing policymakers, businesses, investors, community leaders, and nonprofit organizations to come together and exchange ideas on how to achieve economic, environmental, and human sustainability goals; educates companies and communities on emerging sustainability trends and best practices; and lobbies at the local, state, and national level to formulate and implement policies to encourage sustainability in business. The USGCC website features access to the organization's newsletter, which offers information on recent initiatives and other topics of interest.

**The Carol and Lawrence Zicklin Center
for Business Ethics Research**
The Wharton School, University of Pennsylvania
600 Jon M. Huntsman Hall, 3730 Walnut Street
Philadelphia, PA   19104
(215) 898-7689 • fax: (215) 573-2006
e-mail: lgst-info@wharton.upenn.edu
website: lgst.wharton.upenn.edu

The Carol and Lawrence Zicklin Center for Business Ethics Research is a research center that funds and promotes influential scholarship on business ethics and private sector accountability. Its faculty members are regarded as leaders in the field and frequently present their research at high-profile conferences around the world. In 2007 it launched a partnership with the Center for Political Accountability in Washington, DC, to strengthen corporate political accountability. Its website offers access to a range of its research and information on its upcoming events.

Bibliography of Books

Guler Aras and David Crowder — *Governance and Social Responsibility: International Perspectives.* New York: Palgrave Macmillan, 2012.

Brent D. Beal — *Corporate Social Responsibility: Definition, Core Issues, and Recent Developments.* Los Angeles: SAGE, 2014.

John R. Boatright — *Ethics and the Conduct of Business,* 6th ed. Upper Saddle River, NJ: Pearson Prentice Hall, 2009.

David Bubna-Litic, ed. — *Spirituality and Corporate Social Responsibility: Interpenetrating Worlds.* Burlington, VT: Gower, 2009.

Tom Cannon — *Corporate Responsibility: Governance, Compliance, and Ethics in a Sustainable Environment,* 2nd ed. New York: Pearson, 2012.

Archie B. Carroll, Kenneth J. Lipartito, James E. Post, Patricia H. Werhane — *Corporate Responsibility: The American Experience.* Cambridge: Cambridge University Press, 2012.

Gerald F. Cavanaugh — *American Business Ethics: A Global Perspective.* Upper Saddle River, NJ: Pearson Prentice Hall, 2010.

W. Timothy Coombs and Sherry J. Holladay — *Managing Corporate Responsibility: Communication Approach.* Malden, MA: Wiley-Blackwell, 2012.

Colin Crouch and Camilla Maclean, eds.	*The Responsible Corporation in a Global Economy.* New York: Oxford University Press, 2011.
Mara Einstein	*Compassion, Inc.: How Corporate America Blurs the Line Between What We Buy, Who We Are, and Those We Help.* Berkeley: University of California Press, 2012.
Peter J. Fleming and Marc T. Jones	*The End of Corporate Social Responsibility: Crisis & Critique.* London: SAGE, 2013.
Christine A. Hemingway	*Corporate Social Entrepreneurship: Integrity Within.* Cambridge: Cambridge University Press, 2013.
Bryan Horrigan	*Corporate Social Responsibility in the 21st Century: Debates, Models, and Practices Across Government, Law, and Business.* Northampton, MA: Edward Elgar, 2010.
Philip Kotler, David Hessekiel, and Nancy R. Lee	*Good Works!: Marketing and Corporate Initiatives That Build a Better World—and the Bottom Line.* Hoboken, NJ: Wiley, 2012.
Janet Morrison	*International Business: Challenges in a Changing World.* New York: Palgrave Macmillan, 2009.
Dina Rajak	*In Good Company: An Anatomy of Corporate Social Responsibility.* Stanford, CA: Stanford University Press, 2011.

Lisa Ann Richey and Stefano Ponte
Brand Aid: Shopping Well to Save the World. Minneapolis: University of Minnesota Press, 2011.

Justine Simpson and John Taylor
Corporate Governance, Ethics, and CSR. London: Kogan Page, 2013.

Sarah A. Soule
Contention and Corporate Social Responsibility. New York: Cambridge University Press, 2009.

Richard A. Spinello
Global Capitalism, Culture, and Ethics. New York: Routledge, 2014.

Fiona Starr
Corporate Responsibility for Cultural Heritage: Conservation, Sustainable Development, and Corporate Reputation. New York: Routledge, 2013.

Ralph Tench
Corporate Social Irresponsibility: A Challenging Concept. Bingley, UK: Emerald, 2012.

William B. Werther and David Chandler, Jr.
Strategic Corporate Social Responsibility: Stakeholders in a Global Environment, 2nd ed. Los Angeles: SAGE, 2011.

Jonathan A. Westover, ed.
Socially Responsible and Sustainable Business around the Globe: The New Age of Corporate Social Responsibility. Champaign, IL: Common Ground, 2013.

Olivier F. Williams
Corporate Social Responsibility: The Role of Business in Sustainable Development. New York: Routledge, 2013.

Index